ADVANCE PRAISE

Are you a woman who wants to create the life you have always dreamed of? Then grab a copy of Boot Straps & Bra Straps and enjoy this guidebook by one of the top female mentors, Sheila Mac. As you read this gem of a book, you will learn the BOOTS Formula that will help you create a new identity, reinvent yourself, and produce more income while having a balanced life. Grab a copy of the book for your best friends, too!

TERRI LEVINE, BESTSELLING AUTHOR OF *TURBOCHARGE* AND *TURBOCHARGE YOUR BUSINESS*, WWW.HEARTREPRENEUR.COM

Sheila Mac writes the words of hope and, most importantly, the language of recovery.

One must and should continually take a long look at the ups or downs of one's life journey. Ms. Mac shows you the How, in a constructive, brilliant, and compassionate way. At times it takes darkness and the bitter confinement of one's fear, loneliness, and lowliness to begin the process of learning. "Hold a steady course," wise men tell you; alas, it is not always easy, stumbling blocks come upon us, and that is when we feel lost and incapable of pulling up our "Boot Straps." That will be the time to pick up Sheila Mac's book. When you finish reading it, you will be once again humming playful tunes and shedding joyful tears, most importantly you will find YOU again.

LADY ALIZIA GUR SCHRAGER, CFA PRESIDENT

When Sheila Mac tells you to pull up your boot straps and bra straps, do it! Sheila is the mentor every woman needs, from new mamas to seasoned businesswomen; she will do for you what she has done for so many: guide you from starting over to creating the life you always desired.

PATRICK COMBS, BESTSELLING AUTHOR, CO-FOUNDER OF BLISS CHAMPIONS, AND KEYNOTE SPEAKER, WWW.PATRICKCOMBS.COM

Readers will walk away both inspired and with the right tools in hand to do an entire lifestyle redesign.

DR. GREG REID, AUTHOR OF THE *THINK AND GROW RICH* SERIES

Sheila's voice is that of a strategist, mentor, and loving friend who will hold you accountable with truth and love. Enjoy this book as a guide and share it with a friend or family member going through a tough spot in life. Sheila walks the reader through her solid formula, which touches on how it can help with life's waves such as grief, divorce, relationship struggles, addictions, abuse, elder care, and parenting. As she guides you through the BOOTS Formula, it's as if Sheila is holding your hand and guiding you on to the next right action steps. The book helps you to pick yourself up from rock bottom, reorganize your life, and reinvent yourself, as well as truly live life on your own terms.

JONATHAN KEIM, CEO OF KOKOLATO

If Sheila Mac tells you to pull up your boot straps and bra straps, get ready to take action! In Boot Straps & Bra Straps, Sheila Mac shows you how to use her BOOTS Formula to supercharge yourself and go from starting over to creating the life you always desired.

JAN MORAN, BESTSELLING AUTHOR OF *SEABREEZE INN*, WWW.JANMORAN.COM

Sheila Mac will get your life back into action, no matter what your rock bottom. She is the mentor every woman needs, from new mums to seasoned grandmothers; she will guide you from starting over to creating the life you always desired. A compelling page turner, full of tips, life lessons, and practical insights, Sheila's story, "From struggle to success," plus so many other solid examples, will inspire you.

MARILYN DEVONISH, THE NEUROSUCCESS™COACH, TRANCEFORMATIONS™, WWW.TRANCEFORMATIONSTM.COM

In this excellent book, Sheila Mac has created a clear and powerful path for women in all phases of life to overcome life's bold challenges and become the better version of themselves.

ROBERT ROBOTTI, AUTHOR, *THE SENIOR SEASON* (AMAZON BOOKS)

Sheila's voice is that of a mentor, life coach, and entrepreneur all rolled up into a best friend. This book is a guidebook where she walks the reader through the BOOTS Formula: Sheila's secret tool for those who wish to pick themselves up from any rockbottom situation, build a new identity, and reinvent themselves, as well as produce more income, all without jeopardizing a life of harmony.

HAVILAH MALONE, CEO OF PROOF OF WHAT'S POSSIBLE, INC., WWW.HAVILAHMALONE.COM

Enjoy this book by one of the leading mentors on rebooting one's life. Sheila uses examples that everyone can relate to, as well as become inspired by. This book details the signs of rock bottoming, and we can relate to that. In fact, I don't think this is just for women.

LYNN ROCKSTAD, PRESIDENT, RESPONSIBLE GLOBAL ENERGY, LLC.; FOUNDER/PRESIDENT, ADULT CARE PLACEMENTS, INC., WWW.ADULTCAREPRO.COM

I'm excited that you get to share a piece of Sheila through her book. She is an extremely powerful, positive person who has so much to offer! I am confident this book will help you on your journey, and I believe you will find Sheila as inspirational and informative as I do.

STEVE KEEFER, VETERAN, ENTREPRENEUR, AND OWNER OF U.S. ELITE LLC AND CROSSFIT SOAR

You will want to gift a copy of this book to your closest friend and keep one on the shelf for future life reviews. Sheila is an authentic mentor and a cherished guide. This book is not just for women; it has examples everyone can relate to. Readers won't just walk away inspired; they will walk away with the right tools in hand to do an entire lifestyle redesign.

CHARLES FISHER, CEO SAIFE

BOOT STRAPS

& BRA STRAPS

THE FORMULA TO GO FROM ROCK BOTTOM
BACK INTO **ACTION IN ANY SITUATION**

SHEILA MAC

LIONCREST

PUBLISHING

BOOT STRAPS & BRA STRAPS

The Formula to Go from Rock Bottom Back into Action in Any Situation

ISBN 978-1-5445-0676-0 *Hardcover*

978-1-5445-0674-6 *Paperback*

978-1-5445-0675-3 *Ebook*

978-1-5445-0733-0 *Audiobook*

PUBLISHER'S CATALOGING-IN-PUBLICATION DATA

(Prepared by The Donohue Group, Inc.)

Names: Mac, Sheila, 1969- author.

Title: Boot straps & bra straps : the formula to go from rock bottom back into action in any situation / Sheila Mac.

Other Titles: Boot straps and bra straps

Description: [Austin, Texas] : Lioncrest Publishing, [2020]

Identifiers: ISBN 9781544506760 (hardcover) | ISBN 9781544506746 (paperback) | ISBN 9781544506753 (ebook)

Subjects: LCSH: Women--Psychology. | Motivation (Psychology) | Self-actualization (Psychology) in women. | Stress management for women.

Classification: LCC HQ1206 .M33 2020 (print) | LCC HQ1206 (ebook) | DDC 155.33391--dc23

In memory of Michael Machuca, beloved son of Sheila Mac.

June 2, 1996–December 21, 2019.

My dear family and friends,

I wrote this book for you.

In each person's lifetime, there will be a series of waves or rock-bottom events. I hope that your life is always blessed, and you will never need a guide; however, if you need help and I'm not here, I hope this book will be like having me by your side. It may be that you will need to take it down from the upper shelf, dust it off, and get yourself or a loved one back into action. Know that I will be with you through this book and in spirit as you bravely reboot your life.

As always, I wish you,

"Life, Love, Laughter & Light!"

—Sheila Mac

CONTENTS

INTRODUCTION

Hitting rock bottom can take you by surprise.

It's like you're getting cooked alive—and you don't even feel the heat until you look down and see that you're in hot water. Life was going great, and then the "shift" hit the fan: a surprise rock-bottom event hit you *hard*! Maybe you were fired unexpectedly. Maybe you're facing the sudden death of a loved one. You may be going through a divorce that caught you off guard.

Whatever your personal rock-bottom situation, you weren't prepared for it to happen—at least, not now. Maybe in twenty years, but it certainly wasn't supposed to happen *today*.

A few unaligned choices led you down the wrong road. All of a sudden you look around and think, "Wait a minute, what happened to my life? How the hell did I get to this point?"

And now you feel lost. Scared. Alone.

How are you going to handle this?

On the one hand, you may not want to burden other people, even your friends, with what's going on, so you paint a happier picture than your current reality. You're afraid to reach out and say, "I'm drowning over here, can you help me? I don't know what to do!"

On the other hand, you're not sure what your options are, so you may turn to your friends and family. You are going to hear so many opinions, but just because it sounds like a great idea coming from someone else doesn't mean it aligns with your soul. Your mom, sister, friends, or Aunt Betty may have a prescription for how you should get through this—but if it doesn't feel right to you, it doesn't matter.

You may not have the resources you need to make it through this situation. If you haven't walked down this road before, you may not be sure what steps you need to take, so you feel over-whelmed—in addition to the roller coaster of other emotions you are going through.

To make matters even worse, you're not sleeping much, up all night with insomnia. There isn't time to socialize. Your wellness routine has slowed or stopped. You couldn't even take a walk today because one more urgent thing came up that had to be solved *right now*.

You're exhausted. You're in survival mode. Your decisions about what to do are not going to be sound, because they're coming from a very tired, cranky person.

Let me be very clear: this is an emergency, and you need to be resuscitated. You need a guide to show you how we get through a situation like this, to give you resources, and to help you get out of the emotional pea-soup fog of dealing with a crisis and the resulting fallout.

I've been there, and I'm here to help you.

OUT OF THE FOG

If you weren't emotionally bound up in your situation, you would have more clarity. You would be able to see your best options for dealing with whatever comes up. If the version of yourself who has already walked through this rock bottom and come out the other side could go back in time and give you—the *you* right now—some advice, what would she say?

Would she tell you to slow down, to stop rushing, that you don't have to have all the answers today? Would future you recommend not making any major decisions without reviewing them first, particularly while you're still in the fog? Would she tell you that "normal" is going to look different for a while—but that you *will* feel normal again?

In case we haven't invented time travel by the time you read this book, I'm here to tell you all of the above. I developed the BOOTS Formula to help you learn to make choices, have a life shift, and make great things happen based on your individual values and best life vision.

A change is going to happen, and it's worth it. There is a stage where it feels like everyone in your life is picking at you. Life itself may seem like it's trying its best to stop you from doing whatever you want to do. All you hear is, "*That's a stupid idea*" and "*That's never going to work*" and "*Who do you think you are?*"

One of the hardest things for people to do is to realign and possibly walk away from anything and anyone that conflicts with their value systems—but you are going to discover that power within yourself. Through the activities and examples in this book, you will discover your true north and will be able to easily do what is needed to move forward with your life. Anything that hurts you, that doesn't resonate for you, that fights against what you want and believe in—you are going to give it the BOOT.

Once you have turned your rock-bottom moment into a positive, beautiful life shift, you can live your life on your terms. Your life will probably look different, but you get to design it this time. You are taking your life back—and *you* are in charge, not anybody else.

Sooner than you can imagine, you'll be in the career of your dreams or the relationship you always wanted. Because you are going to learn to develop healthy boundaries, because you are going to do things differently along the way from here to there, you will begin to attract the people, the job, the place to live, all of the opportunities that align with who you are—your essence, your truth, not anybody else's or even society's expectations of the way you're supposed to be.

Once you have accepted that you are in charge of living your life, and you begin to embody living your truth, people are going to see *you*. They're going to be inspired by *you*. Then, you're going to hear, "Hey, can you show me how you did that? I want to do it, too!"

When you assess your peer group and up-level according to your life purpose and vision, and once you have created a life shift for yourself—whatever that looks like—your life is not just full; it's fulfilled. Not only do you get more—and better—sleep, you wake up rested and happy. You know that you're doing what you need to do.

Yes, sometimes your heart will call you to leave certain friends or family members, in order to find a more aligned peer group. From what I have seen, however, the ones who leave always return to lead their family and friends to success! Because your friends are more in alignment with your beliefs and value system, they support you while also pushing you toward your personal best. Life still involves work but, as a whole, it feels far more effortless.

But you don't have to wait for the right person, right job, or right investment opportunity to show up. You can start living now so that every moment as you go forward through the process of recovering from rock bottom and redesigning your life is one more step to being that best version of you, the one who came back to guide you now.

You are going to walk out of your tough spot one small step at a time—and that's what this book is going to help with: choosing the next small action steps that you can actually take, even when things feel overwhelming. Because you have had the experience of getting through this rock-bottom moment, you will know that you are strong enough to get through anything.

I've had more than one of my own rock bottoms and come out the other side. Let me tell you about my first.

THE DESCENT

I was eighteen when I got a huge surprise: I was pregnant with my son, my first child. (That was *not* my rock-bottom moment. Each of my children—I now have six, three of my own and three foster-to-adopt—is a blessing.) I was young, expecting a little one, and I had to figure out my life—fast.

While I was pregnant, I took a computer programming class at the local community college. Then, at the beginning of my second trimester, I got a kidney infection. The baby's dad and his family brought me to the hospital—and they left me there when they heard the doctor say that I had blood poisoning and needed an emergency abortion or I might not survive through the night.

In my family's religion, I was raised to believe that abortion wasn't an option, and I thought that the hospital didn't want to try to save the baby because I didn't have insurance. I was sick with a high temperature and yelling at my doctors while refusing to sign the form to agree to the procedure. Just then a woman walked by, an intern, and said, "Why don't we try this new drug, Cipro?"

The doctors were all angry with the intern, and with me, but we agreed to give the new drug a try.

Looking back, I suppose the doctors were trying to help me make a life-altering decision using my infection as a very plausible excuse. They witnessed my boyfriend and his family walking away once they announced my grave situation. Being a young mother with little to no support or family is a tough journey, and medically my body was being poisoned. I very well could have died that night.

During that critical time, the doctors tried to save my son's life and mine. Sadly, my boyfriend and his family left me there to die without even saying goodbye. They never came back to the hospital—not until close to when my son was born. (My boyfriend eventually came back into my life and I later married him—for all the wrong reasons—but that comes in a future chapter.)

I felt all alone on the planet. I hadn't talked to my family in years, I had spent the prior eight years homeless or in the foster care system, and my friends were too young to fully grasp the situation. I sat there scared to live on and terrified that I may die with no one by my side. *What did I ever do to be so unlovable?* I wondered.

The truth was, I wanted desperately to live and to be loved, but I was too scared to have a pity party, as my life and that of my child's could be over before morning. I had this knowing that I needed to stay prayerful and positive to ensure that the drug worked.

And it did.

My blood levels became safe, and I was happy that they didn't have to abort my baby. The doctors told me that because the kidney infection was so bad and it was a high-risk pregnancy, I would have to stay in the hospital for a few months.

I was put in a shared room and all of a sudden, I finally wasn't alone anymore. My roommate, Shirley, had been a bus driver for the city of Los Angeles. She was tough and a bit salty. When I filled her in on my situation, she told me what she would do to that boyfriend and his family if they ever showed up.

We became instant friends as we both had only each other. Although Shirley had a few family members visit, for the most part she was roughing the hospital trip alone as well.

One day, however, the doctors announced that Shirley was well enough to be released. I had the room to myself, and in that moment, I had to make a choice about what was going to happen next and how I was going to show up for myself and my baby. I decided that I was not going to let anybody else be lonely in that hospital. I was going to be there for those other people.

I noticed so many patients didn't have family visiting them either! Even the youngest children were sometimes alone. I walked around and talked to the other patients all day. The nurses showed me how to give them juice or water depending on the person's medical needs. I guess I adopted them all and found that by giving love away with no expectation, I received love in return. That choice—deciding to help other people—is what healed me and got me through those difficult times.

HITTING BOTTOM

My son was born very sick and almost died. He had severe sinus and ear infections from birth and those moments, cradling his hot body in the hospital as he shook with fever-induced convulsions and the doctors had to place him in ice to bring down his temperature—that was my rock bottom.

Because I had been in the hospital for three months, obviously I hadn't been able to go to work. I had been living in a converted garage in East L.A. and I was just barely able to get by without losing everything I had.

I knew that I had to get back to work in order to pay for health insurance for both of us. I was so young, and I didn't feel that I had a lot of resources or help that I could turn to, so I had to figure that "shift" out for myself.

I had to start over, from rock bottom.

I finished my programming certificate at community college. I got extra student loans in order to get through and rent another small place. Sometimes, food was a luxury. One week, I only had a jar of peanut butter and a bag of oranges to eat. I was so grateful when a friend invited me over for dinner!

NASA's Jet Propulsion Lab posted a job opening for a beginning programmer, a position that came with both healthcare benefits and a bonus to cover childcare, and I *needed* that job. It was the highest-paying position I could get at the time, from a young mother's perspective.

I wasn't the best student, but I got the job—because I was the only one who went in and applied for it. Everybody else's attitude was, "You can't apply at JPL; that's for geniuses. There's no way they'll hire me." That's when I learned that the secret is to always ask—sometimes, that's all it takes!

Less than a month after my son was born, I started working again.

I hated seeing my child suffer through these life-threatening ordeals. I couldn't provide everything that I wanted for my young baby. But that pushed me to go get the best possible job I could get, with the training I had, to make sure his needs were met and we could get better health insurance. I was willing to climb every mountain to give this kid my best.

I didn't love the computer programming job, but I did well at it. My son, however, kept getting sick. He attended a subsidized daycare and preschool program, but they would let sick children come in. My son's immune system wasn't very strong, and he caught infection after infection.

Once or twice a month, I would have to rush him to the hospital for treatment. We would spend four or five nights there before it was safe to take him home again. I was exhausted from pulling all-nighters at the hospital, and I wanted my son to be in a place where he wouldn't keep getting sick.

All those hospital visits cost money. Because of the ear infections, my little one's hearing wasn't very good, and he needed speech therapy, which cost more money. I needed to move him out of that daycare, and I needed to make more money than what the government job was paying at JPL.

I had to take a risk.

Leaving that job meant that I had to find another position that had healthcare benefits and allowed me to pay for the quality childcare I needed to provide the best for my child.

I transferred to a job at the phone company. My shift was late, three o'clock until midnight, but it provided healthcare and a better paycheck. I worked overtime and holidays that nobody else wanted to work so I could save up to do something different. During the day, I was a teacher's assistant at my son's new school, in trade for discounted school tuition.

In my spare time—when it was slow at work or before falling

asleep—I would shop for used items to sell on the side. I went to garage sales and dug through the offerings, looking for things that could be fixed up and resold. I spent hours at antique stores hunting for hidden bargains and started going to auctions at storage facilities. Back then we didn't have the internet, so I spent weekends taking items to sell at the local swap meets. After a while, I was earning as much money at this side hustle as I made at my full-time job.

Finally, I took the little bit of savings that I had, and I opened my own gift store.

I negotiated to get a 4,500-square-foot store in Montrose, California. I had six months of free rent to help with tenant improvement costs. I continued going to garage sales, auctions, and storage units and bought their contents at a discount to sell at the store.

I was already well versed in negotiations, so I would go to the tradeshows and arrange to buy an entire wholesale booth's inventory. Whatever I couldn't sell in my store went to the swap meet. I made sure to listen to what my clients wanted and then ordered accordingly. I was also lucky to have an eye for things and would often double or triple my money. That store became a very successful business venture.

Part of me felt like I was still in that rock-bottom place because I saw all my friends acting like the young people we were. They were still in school, preparing to graduate from high school or just starting their first year of college, having fun. They went to parties, while I was this young, serious mom who could never do that because it wasn't the example I wanted for my child.

EMPOWERED AT LAST

After a few months, I didn't have to work a second job anymore—and I was ready to bring in employees to help me even more.

I hired mothers who wanted time with their babies—so I hired nannies, too. The mothers could see their babies and take them for walks in the park, and the nannies were with them while the moms became star salespeople. They just needed flex time, working for someone who understood the demands of what it means to be a working mother.

I wanted to give back to the community, so I also hired kids who were in the foster care system and who were emancipating soon. They were paid by the government through the Job Training Partnership Act. I created a training program for the students, filming every aspect of running a store. They got paid to have pizza and soda, watch the videos, and then work their way through the different levels from cleaning to sales. At the end, I gave them a letter of recommendation so that they could get a better job.

I'm confident that this heart-centered approach to my business is why it was so successful. People feel your intentions, and I wanted to help people and give back.

It was a great experience, and my life shifted within a couple of years. My son went to a better school, and we had a nanny helping out because I could pay for that with the income from the store.

Since then I've made investments in real estate, earned a business and teaching degree, and raised a family. In many ways, everything fell into place.

Don't get me wrong, there were still lots of ups and downs. It wasn't happily ever after—but nobody's real life ends with those words. These patterns show up over and over again.

But when you keep showing up, you discover your calling. Your mission. Your gift in life. You can't hide purpose; it just keeps showing up. If you try to fight it, it will keep knocking you off track until you find the right path. It will keep pushing you, and you will think, "Damn, I hit another rock bottom." Why? Because your soul-calling is getting you onto what you're really here to do. And it will get more and more painful until you really start to listen, until you see the beautiful possibilities— until you realize that you are living life on your own terms and sharing your unique gifts with the world.

Only after we've made it through and come out the other side stronger can we learn what it takes to make an empowering life shift—and to give other people a boost when they get stuck.

TRY THIS ON FOR SIZE

Just like a pair of boots—or a bra for that matter—this book isn't one size fits all. I'm not going to tell you the exact steps you need to do to get out of your specific situation or to make your life better. Instead, I'm going to offer you a formula that can be applied to *any* situation, one that will help you see the next step to take to design your own beautiful life shift.

This isn't a vitamin that makes you feel a little bit better; it's the medication that saves your life.

If you are going through something right now, you can read chapter one to get an overview of what the BOOTS Formula is and how it works, and then you can go to the chapter that discusses something similar to what you may be going through.

Particularly as you are struggling, it may seem overwhelming to think that you have to read twelve chapters before you learn the next steps to take. You don't have to! You can learn the very first step to take right away. Each chapter will give you information that you can implement right now, not something that you may find useful somewhere down the line. Jump to what appeals, the topic that is calling out to you, whatever you need to help you through your situation.

But then go back and review the other chapters, so you can see how it all fits together and how these patterns can happen in anything you're going through. Come back and read chapter 11 on Lifestyle Design, because that applies to everyone.

Each chapter has a similar structure: it tells the story of a woman going through a specific real-life rock-bottom situation, it discusses things you can do to avoid that type of rock bottom, and it shows you how to address the rock bottom if you end up in a similar situation. You will then see a breakdown of the BOOTS Formula for that situation, as well as the moment of empowerment found by the woman in the opening story.

At the very end of each chapter, you will find an activity and links to more resources you can use to do the work, but it will also link you to a community of like-minded women who are going through similar situations. Finally, in the Directory of Resources at the end of the book, you will see examples from my "Dear Sheila" newsletter, for even more illustrations of women learning to walk through their own rock-bottom moments, to inspire you to keep going through yours.

This is a guide, not something to read and then throw away. You're going to want to give it to the women in your life, but you'll want to keep a copy for yourself to refer back to. There are guidelines and tips throughout. It's a tool that gives different models and examples that can all spark ideas—ideas that come from you. It's going to draw out your own strength and your ideas of what the life you are designing—or redesigning—is going to look like.

When you make it through this situation, you will be prepared for whatever life has in store for you next.

BLUEPRINTS TO REBUILD

Why did you pick up this book?

Do you need to reinvent your life? Are you barreling toward a rock-bottom moment of your own? Have you already hit rock bottom and now you're struggling to stand up and take that first shaky step toward rebuilding what "normal" looks like? Are you tired of revisiting rehabs or falling down over and over again, and now you're ready for a complete reboot?

Maybe you don't even think you're at rock bottom. You're just not satisfied with your life and you want to redesign it. Maybe you're ready to jump into the next chapter of your life. You've already declared, "Enough is enough!" and now you're ready to take back your power.

You've invested your life in a relationship, your children, your career, and now you're ready for a life shift, but you need direction. This book is a guide that will give you that direction. You'll see that other women and I have gone through this stuff—and if we can make it through, so can you.

The details of our situations don't have to be exactly the same. We all share the circumstance of hitting rock bottom and having to decide how we choose to move forward and get through that first—of many—life shifts by making it a positive, intentional one.

There are a lot of steps that go into this formula. You don't just go from the hospital to opening a store the next day. There are a hell of a lot of steps in between. If you're ready to find *your* moment of empowerment, turn the page to learn how the BOOTS Formula can guide you on your way.

CHAPTER 1

OVERVIEW OF THE BOOTS FORMULA

In December of 2017, I lost my house, my car, and my cat due to a fire. (It sounds like a country music song, but that was my reality—and yet another rock-bottom situation after a long period of doing really well.)

I had just finalized a divorce, purchased a new car, and moved into a house that I bought for myself and one of my kids to live in while she went to college. I put all of my savings into it, closed escrow on November 3, and spent some time making it beautiful—more for my kid than myself. I was cash poor but proud to finally get into a nice home again.

A month later, I had a late meeting with a client and was then called to check on an issue with a vacation rental cabin I was running up in the hills. I was frustrated with the delay, thinking, "I'm so tired, and I've been working so hard. I just want to go home to my new place and sleep."

Later, I realized that delay was a protection and I was grateful for the soul reroute, even if it was initially beyond my understanding.

As I drove back, I saw the flames of the huge Thomas Fire in Ventura that ended up burning for close to a month and spread over 280,000 acres. The hills near my house were burning. Twenty-foot flames leapt into the air, which was thick with choking, black smoke and soot. I felt sick to my stomach when I saw the extent of the fire.

As I got closer, I was told that I had to evacuate my home. I rescued my cat and got a few things together, but the power was already out so I grabbed paperwork and pictures, anything I could shove into a box in the dark. Some of my neighbors were in denial, refusing to leave until the firefighters came through issuing mandatory evacuations. They thought it was a little fire over in the hills. They hadn't been on my drive home; they didn't know it was one of the biggest fires in California history and the largest I'd ever seen in my life.

I drove back to the little prefab mobile home that I was renting out through a vacation rental service. One of the units was empty, but it wasn't finished. It had a toilet and a kitchen, but it didn't have a shower or many of the other things it needed to make it livable. It was maybe 400 square feet, and that's where I unloaded all the boxes of stuff that were now my only earthly possessions.

The next day, one of my friends came over to help me and when she opened the door, the cat I had rescued ran out the door. She was so freaked out by the move that she just bolted and never came back. We couldn't find her, even with a microchip.

Shortly after that, my car was totaled in an accident, and my descent to rock bottom was complete. But this time I was able to get back into action in record time, using a formula I had learned from all the other waves in life.

THE BOOTS FORMULA

I've had an interesting life. It hasn't been easy, but I'm not complaining—and I'm not a victim. I've had a lot of rock bottoms, a lot of downs but a lot of ups as well—I mean, how many ten-year-olds get to meet the president? (I'll tell you that story later in the book!) Through it all, I had to learn how to go from rock bottom to rock solid.

I had to look back at what I've done—and what I still do—to get out of that place and back into life. I asked myself, "What has helped me walk through the bottom faster and still be who I want to be—without letting it totally screw up my life?"

What did I do last time, and how did I do it? What type of a mindset did I need to have? Who did I need to reach out to? Who did I need to be?

I saw the patterns in all the times I've had to do that—and in how I've seen my friends and clients get through their rock-bottom moments as well. Ultimately, I came up with the BOOTS Formula, a simple yet powerful method of redirecting your thoughts and actions. The BOOTS Formula will teach you the skills you need to quickly dissolve limiting beliefs and get back into action.

In simple language? BOOTS will grab your problem by the bra straps and help you get back into action in any situation.

Sound like something you can use? Let's take a look at each letter.

B IS FOR BEING

The first letter of the BOOTS Formula is B, which stands for Being. At one point in my life, I decided, "This is who I'm being in all that I'm doing."

When "shift" has hit the fan, you realize, "This is messy," and you just have to roll up your sleeves. Maybe you have other people to help you, but maybe you don't. Either way, you have to be the one in command. You have to decide who you're being and what you're doing. Whether you're starting over or just hoping to make it through, you have to ask yourself, *"How am I going to show up through this?"*

Who are you going to be as you're walking your puppies or cleaning up the mess? Who are you going to be while you're reorganizing your life and changing your living situation? If you're being who you really are, then you won't be in that bad situation for long.

This first letter in the BOOTS Formula—B for Being—shows up in how you're speaking, having fun with family and friends, or helping a client. Who you choose to be while doing all that you're required to do as you move from rock bottom back into action makes all the difference.

But why is this so important? Because the way you show up and the energy that comes from you will help attract better things in your life. I know that sounds like magic, but it's happened to me time and again, as you'll see throughout the book.

The opposite is true as well—if you show up with negative energy, you will attract worse things into your life.

You'll notice that when you meet people who focus only on the negative, everything that comes out of their mouth is complaints, tragedy, and chaos. Somehow, these things just *happen* to them. And this becomes a pattern. Those people are training their subconscious mind to look for the negatives to show up, so they don't even see the positives.

But when we're able to retrain our minds to focus on the positives, we're able to enjoy more of life—even while we're rebuilding and rebooting. We're going to starve those negative thoughts, not feeding them with our attention, time, or energy. When you focus on the good parts of your life, those things that you can be grateful for in this moment, that energy will bring even more good things your way.

Don't get me wrong—you still have to take the action steps to get out of the negative, and you're going to have times in your life when you're just going to have to do whatever's in front of you. It may not be the prettiest thing to do, but it doesn't matter.

Sometimes, when you're focusing on getting out of a hole, it feels like you're buried in your own self-centric thinking. But when you can get out of that mindset and put down your problem for a moment, it clears the way for a solution. One way to do this is to help someone less fortunate than you—volunteering with your community, religious organization, school, or work—which allows you to fully show up, contribute, and utilize your unique talents. When you're using your flow, you're not thinking about the problem at hand. You're not showing up for approval. You're just being your best self.

If you're showing up and being fully present, people will see your true essence and respond to that. Having that respite will open a floodgate of ideas and give you the resources to resolve any difficult situation you find yourself in.

This first letter is a reminder to stay in your Being and live your truth. It will help you stay grounded and centered when things are in a state of change and chaos. The truth is that there's often form, freedom, and order even in the center of a storm.

THE FIRST O IS FOR ORIENTATION

The next letter in the BOOTS Formula stands for Orientation. As you are living through your rock-bottom moment, you need to know that it's not better than it is, and it's not worse than it is; it just *is what it is*.

Assessing your current Orientation is a really big action step in the BOOTS process. Discovering Orientation is part of the overall change you may be in, and it will help you find some surprisingly simple solutions.

In this case, we're referring to a place. Where do you find yourself on the map of your life? Within this stage, you'll also acknowledge where you were in the past and where you want to be. Once you know where "here" is, you can answer "how did I get here?" and "where do I want to go from here?"

Assessing your Orientation also means considering your options and saying, "I am here on the map. I want to go over there." You need to know where you are in order to think about how to take the next step. If you want to go from California to New York, you first have to know you're starting from California. You then have to know that to get there, "I can walk, I can swim, I can jog, I can take a flight, or I can take a bike, I can take a bus, or I can take a train."

You use your rock bottom to set the direction for your life *beyond* this rock-bottom situation.

It's important that you are really honest about where you are in this situation. You can't lie, because you don't want to give up your personal responsibility. You have to own every part of this and realize it could be worse, it could be better, but this is it. If you aren't able to be honest about where you're starting from, you won't be able to clearly see where you want to go or how to get there. If you're not realistic about that first point of Orientation, it's almost impossible to get out of your rock-bottom moment—at the very least, it will take a hell of a lot longer.

A lot of people have a hard time accepting the truth of where they are. They might think, "Oh, I'm kind of here, but I wish I was there." No, this is where you are. This is where you're starting from. That may be where you want to go, but you won't get there if you don't know where you are on the map.

The last piece of Orientation is owning it. You are responsible for where you are now. The minute you start blaming people or situations outside of yourself—it was my mother's fault, my brother's fault, the weather's fault—guess who's in control of your life? Everyone but you.

When you own your situation, however, you're taking back your power: "Damn, yes, I spent that money." Or, "Oops, I did trash that credit card—but I'm not going to blame Macy's or Nordstrom. I'm just going to have to do something different here."

Nobody else gets to be in charge of your life; from here on, you own it.

Once you've gone through the Orientation process, you'll get a grounding sense of peace and clarity, and you'll be able to acknowledge just how far you've already traveled. Give yourself some credit! Admit that you may have messed up in one area, but also look at the good parts of where you are.

Once you have the answer to, "How the hell did this happen to me?" your next question is probably, "How can I ever unravel this mess and get back into action?"

The next letter of BOOTS will help you answer that.

THE SECOND O IS FOR ORDER OF OPERATIONS

The third step of the BOOTS Formula is finding the Order of Operations. When you are in a rock-bottom moment, there are certain steps you know you need to take to get out of it—and you need to complete those steps in a certain order, which will be different depending on what you're going through. Throughout the book, I'll show you these steps in other, specific rock-bottom situations. As you learn the steps for yourself, you'll become adept at facing any other rock bottom you may find yourself in.

In the military, they train people to focus on one thing, find and execute the solution, then move on to the next thing, and the next. If you complete tasks on the battlefield in the wrong order, you're not going to win. If you do steps in the wrong order in math, you're not going to get the solution. In algebra, you must follow an ordered set of actions to solve for X, and one step cannot be done without doing the prior calculations. The same is true here; it's very important to order your steps and then complete them *in that order*.

Consider this step your BOOTS-camp, a battle plan for accomplishing things in a certain order so the magic happens.

Each step may take a bit of time, and there will be days when you feel as if nothing has transpired and you've seen absolutely no change. There's lag time while you're completing small tasks, organizing, setting things up, or whatever your steps may be. If you're trying to lose weight, you may think, "I've been working on this diet for a month now; why can't I get into these size-two jeans? What the hell?!"

Then, all of a sudden—if you're really clear on the goal and you're following the path with your Order of Operations—all the lag time catches up, you reach equilibrium between effort and results, and then boom! You're going downhill. It gets easier. You start to see results at a rapid pace: there's less to do, less chaos and stress, and you have some free time.

As you get started figuring out the Order of Operations, it's important to know that everything is not going to happen on the very first day you apply it. It took you a while to get into the mess, so it may take time to get out. Once you start to follow the Order of Operations and you do the work, however, the universal law of momentum takes over and most people arrive at their desired outcome ahead of the expected time.

Now, you're ready to write out important strategy steps that will help you—slowly at first—start taking small action steps each day toward your desired new outcome. And after you complete this strategy session, you will start on the journey to designing the life you choose.

T IS FOR THINKING

The fourth step of the BOOTS Formula is Thinking.

If you recall your Thinking at the most successful points in your life, it's probably vastly different from your Thinking when a crisis brings you to a rock-bottom situation. Often, at the toughest times, our Thinking goes to survival. We lose sight of the possibilities and opportunities that are before us. This is where Thinking comes into play: it's vital to have a strong mindset in order to keep our BOOTS on and walk out of a rough spot in life.

Thinking leads you to a clear vision of where you want to go on that map of your desired outcome. You've made the decision that you're going to New York. Your bags are packed. You have an idea of how you're going to get there—you know the steps you need to take, though you may not know how the hell you're going to take them all—but you've made up your mind: that's where you're going. Tony Robbins often says, "It is in the moment of decision that one's destiny is shaped." That decision is the thought that comes before the action steps required to reach your new goal.

Everything happens in this step, in that decision. You can see it, feel it, embody it. Things start to show up because you're looking for them and you're open to them. You'll start getting the results you want just because that decision is in your mind. It becomes that real to you.

Once you have that clear vision in your mind, you have to see yourself as if you are already living in your desired reality; you're just doing the steps to get there.

S IS FOR STEPPING UP

The fifth and final step of the BOOTS Formula is a literal step: Stepping Up.

You've gone through the first four steps. You've decided how you're going to show up, you have a picture of where you're going, you know the steps you need to take, and you've made the decision to actually do something. It would be nice if you could just sit, think, and meditate your desired outcome into Being—but that's not the way it works.

There is some validity to the idea of manifesting what you want, but at the same time you have to believe enough to actually go out there and take the risk. You have to overcome your fear of giving your first presentation, making your first speech, or writing your first book. You have to get out of your comfort zone. And you have to take those steps.

S is for Stepping Up by taking the personal responsibility required for a real reboot. While the B in BOOTS is about Being in the present with who you are in the situation, S is for taking those steps toward the future you want.

Although there will be many times in life where we have little or no true personal responsibility for an event that alters our lives, it is always a gift to own your own response and reactions to situations. What can you do to shift the energy and step up to your part in the situation? In order to reboot, one must be willing to step into action.

This last step ties back to the first one; it all comes back to Being. How are you going to be when you're going through this? Sometimes it's ugly, dirty, not pretty, and certainly not fun. Nobody's going to help you move, so you have to pack all the boxes yourself. Procrastinating isn't going to help. You just have to take those action steps you defined in the Order of Operations.

When you first start, it's overwhelming because you feel like you're still buried in the situation. Chaos is all around. But because you've done the first four steps of BOOTS, you have an action plan. You're not doing a thousand steps today; you just have to take one. You do the things that you mapped out, one by one, and that helps you see, "Okay, I can do that." You have clarity on the action steps, so now it's time to actually get moving.

Are you ready to strap on your BOOTS and start walking?

FROM ROCK BOTTOM TO MOMENT OF EMPOWERMENT

You may be thinking, "Okay, now I know the formula. But what does it look like in action?"

Great question! Let's look at the rock-bottom moment I told you about at the beginning of the chapter to see how I applied the BOOTS Formula to get back into right action.

After the fire, after my cat ran away, and after my car was totaled, I was in a funk for a week and a half or two weeks before I even noticed. I don't know if it was shock or depression or overwhelm—probably all of that. It was a lot of loss in a short period of time.

But then I had to go back to work—and I needed a way to get there.

BEING

For that first week or two, I was being a victim. I grieved the cat, the car I had recently bought in cash and was very proud of, my house and the whole lifestyle I had just rebuilt after the divorce—another loss that I had recently overcome. All my beautiful, most favorite things were in that house, and I lost them all.

I was also grieving over the plan to have one of my children move back in with me while she went to college. She'd already been having second thoughts, but she didn't want to tell me and risk hurting my feelings. When I ended up in the tiny house in the hills, we both realized it wasn't going to happen.

It felt like a really shitty place to end up. I wondered, "How the hell did I get here in just a five-day period?

As I was going through my own rock-bottom situations, I had to ask, "Who do I need to be?" I had to own my little strength as well as my many weaknesses. I had to be vulnerable enough to admit those weaknesses in order to use my strengths to help me through. I had to own my truth, own myself, and trust that I was going to do the steps to get out of this rock bottom.

I also had to take care of myself. I had a good reason to have a pity party—but I had even better reasons to get out of that funk and start asking, "What can I do?"

When I was showing up with an active mindset instead of the pity party, it made a big difference.

Evacuating from the fire and the immediate aftermath was a terrible situation. I could have blamed the fire—after all, I lost almost everything. But that would have meant giving power to that fire and giving up my own power over the situation. Blaming somebody or something else puts you in the victim role—and I didn't want to be a victim. I didn't want to sit there and feel powerless. I wasn't in control of the fire itself, but I was in control of my reaction to it.

I was in control of how I decided to wake up in the morning, and what I decided to do with each day, how I wanted to move forward.

After the fire, I had to do a big assessment to see where I was financially and to recognize that emotionally I was down the hill. I was shocked and depressed. A lot of my friends had lost their homes, too—and the fires were still burning!

Everybody in the entire community was suffering. We were all affected, somber behind our respirator masks. Schools and businesses were closed, so children stayed home with their parents, who couldn't go to work anyway. People who had lost their homes were relocated to emergency shelters. It was very devastating. I felt for everyone around me—but I was in the middle of it, too.

To orient myself, I had to ask, "What are my options? What are my resources? Who can help me? What can I do to help other people?"

Then, I had to say, "Wow, I have to use that BOOT to kick myself out of this!"

ORDER OF OPERATIONS

It was during this stage of the process that I realized I had to use every single resource that I had.

I had to go through boxes of stuff I rescued from the fire. I had to pay bills and file my insurance claim.

I got a beat-up Nissan, really old and funky, that barely ran. The windows rolled down using a hand crank, and you had to lock the doors manually; nothing was automatic at all. It needed a ton of maintenance, but it just wasn't worth putting money into it. I had to take the car up and down a canyon road, though, so I paid to fix the brakes and steering. While I was waiting for the mechanic to finish, I went and bought a fancy steering wheel cover and a bunch of motivational stickers that I plastered all over the inside of the car. I had it waxed and cleaned and made it the best damn beater car you could drive. I was going to rough it in style.

That was when I started to get out of my funk a little. I knew that I had to focus on the positive, not think about what I had lost, and look instead at what I was going toward.

I couldn't make it down the hill to the gym to work out until the car was fixed, so I got out my old rebounder trampoline and said affirmations while I worked out (which you'll learn about in the exercise at the end of this chapter). The neighbors thought I was crazy!

I let other people who had lost their homes stay in the other units of my home rental, helping people who were just as bad off as I was but who didn't have a mobile home to go to. I made space by sifting through the things I had rescued and donating anything I didn't absolutely need to other people who needed them more than I did.

I felt better helping people than I did sitting around in my pity party. I couldn't get stuck blaming the fire for all my problems. There was nothing I could do to change what had happened— all I could do was figure out how to move forward and up-level by figuring out how to help other people who were affected and even worse off than I was.

Just the act of getting up and doing *something*, being able to contribute and be involved, was empowering.

THINKING

I had to have the thoughts, the vision, of what life could look like.

It was a lot of mind over matter. Any time it got to be too much, thinking about my loss, I said, "That's silly, I don't have time for that." I don't mean to sound like I was always cheerful; I just kept laser focused only on what I could be grateful for: I was alive, I had a roof over my head and a car to drive. My family was safe.

I was still devastated at the loss of my home, my car, my cat, the opportunity to live with my daughter. It wasn't easy for me, but I had a tested formula to follow that got me through it, because this was not my first rock bottom.

I also realized that the strange delays I encountered that day were protecting me. I could have been at home, asleep, while houses burned around me. Instead, I was kept safe. Remember all those soul reroutes that took me off my regular schedule? They were a gift. Staying focused on the positive helped me continue to look for the blessing, the gift, the good part of a bad situation.

I put everything I had into this, because I had to get out of it.

And, eventually, I did.

How I showed up then determined what my life continues to look like. Now, I'm closing escrow on a beautiful house in a wonderful community, writing this book, and helping thousands of people through my consulting and online programs.

A lot can happen in a short period of time, but whether that's a positive or negative has so much to do with your mindset. I could still be up there in that cabin complaining about that fire and wondering where my other shoe ended up. Instead, I took action, determined the steps I needed to take—and eventually went out and bought new shoes.

STEPPING UP

You can't show up in a beater car to show clients around potential homes, so I had to rent a car for my real estate business. That was just one more expense.

When one of the rental cars I was driving broke down, I had to reschedule my appointment with my real estate clients. As I was waiting for the tow truck, I got an email from Hyundai saying to come test drive a car and they'd give me a $40 Visa card. I thought, "Well, the worst that could happen would be getting an extra $40 to put toward all my expenses."

When I got to the lot, among all the Hyundais, I saw one white Mercedes—exactly like the rental I had driven the weekend before for a dear client and friend. It felt good. That car would be perfect for all the driving I did as a real estate agent.

I took the money I'd set aside to repair the clunker car and used it as a down payment. Because the dealership was in an area that didn't sell a lot of Mercedes, they let me have it for well under the Blue Book price. The car was preowned with a good number of miles, but it was a huge blessing to me.

After I bought it, they sent someone out to show me how to use all the buttons. That man looked exactly like my father, who had passed away. As I drove away, I knew I had gotten a little help from Dad and said a silent thank you to him.

Opportunities and solutions show up when you're open to them. You have to have faith, confidence, and a willingness to step up.

YOU CAN DO THIS

Every pair of boots is different, but you can always find a pair that fits you. Similarly, every rock-bottom situation is different—but you can find your own way of applying the BOOTS Formula to fit your needs.

You *can* do this.

You now have a formula to follow, on your own terms.

Each chapter of the rest of the book covers one specific rock-bottom situation. You can jump to the one you really need right now—but come back and do the work, so that the rock-bottom moment you're feeling right now turns into a beautiful life shift.

Activity to Re-BOOT: Mantra for Being

When I found myself in the rock-bottom situation I told you about in this chapter, having lost everything in a fire and jumping on a rebounder for ten minutes at a time, I didn't have anyone else to lean on. I didn't have someone to guide me out of that funky place.

I had to talk myself through the situation, and I did that through affirmations.

Saying affirmations is proclaiming, declaring, or stating something as a fact. It could be something that hasn't happened yet or something you know but haven't lived into fully. When we say these affirmations, our subconscious mind starts to believe them and helps us to live more into having those things actually show up in our lives.

It's not magic—it's neuroscience. By repeating affirmations, you reprogram your mind to focus and affirm the things you want to show up in your life. You're empowering yourself to do what needs to be done. Everybody has ups and downs, and if you're going to try to do a lot of new things, you're going to fall a lot. When you use positive affirmations, you're able to get back up and keep going. It doesn't matter what other people tell us; all that matters is what we're telling ourselves now, because that's going to produce the results that we want.

To get started, you can say these affirmations when you first get up. Have them on your phone or on a card by your bed. Try saying them when you're getting ready for your day or while you're having breakfast, coffee, or tea. Then say them again before you go to bed.

When you run into an obstacle or naysayer, get out your affirmations and read them again. Instead of letting that negativity into your mind, put your own positive words in.

Here are some sample affirmations that you can use to get started. Feel free to adapt them to your own situation. Rewrite them to fit wherever you are in your life right now—or write your own original affirmations!

- "In all I choose to be doing, it is who I'm Being that will make all the difference."
- "Every day in every way, life is guiding me to better and better places."
- "As I find the gift in all that is around me, more and more blessings unfold."
- "I am a lifetime learner and a wisdom earner."
- "I am honoring this day and all the good in it in every way."
- "Today I am proud of these three accomplishments: one, two, and three (list your accomplishments)."

I knew that I *had* to apply affirmations. As I did, more and more good things started showing up. First, I thought, "Wow, that's an interesting coincidence. How serendipitous!"

But when it kept happening more and more, all I could think was, "I'm not giving this up!"

Saying affirmations is one action step you can take immediately.

Another is meditating. As soon as I wake up and before I go to sleep, I meditate.

You may already have a solid meditation or prayer practice in place. Going through a tough spot is the best time to stay consistent in your practice. Even if you feel like you don't have the time, setting aside even a few minutes will help carry you through the BOOTS process, reduce stress, and give your mind and body the gift of resting from the situation at hand.

🎁 My Gift to You 🎁

I want to gift you this www.SheilaMac.com/bootsmeditation.

Whenever you need to unwind and regroup in order to have some space while working through the BOOTS Formula. It helps for grounding and clarity, as well as to attract greater abundance, freedom, and flow in your beautiful, authentic life.

CHAPTER 2

FEEL YOUR FEELINGS (GRIEF)

My dad was diagnosed with cancer and passed away on Father's Day, a few months before my son was born. Three months later, his mother passed away, joining my paternal grandfather who had passed away when I was younger. Six months after my grandmother's death, my maternal grandfather passed away. Then my maternal grandmother, the last of my grandparents, passed away, too.

I lost all these relatives in such a short period of time. I had four gift stores and was getting the fifth up and running. I had just given birth to my youngest child, and I was taking care of the other people who were still alive—and they were grieving, too.

I noticed that my remaining family and our close friends all grieved differently. Some people cried straight-on for a couple of weeks or months, and just really disconnected from society. They went into a complete grieving, like they took a grief vacation. Other people, who had a tendency to drink or use other substances, went off the deep end with their addiction as a coping mechanism. Then they had to get through that backslide and get back on their feet and out of whatever bad habit was brought back into their life.

I had never faced so much death or had anything big to grieve before. I didn't know what to expect of myself or how to process this grief and sadness. I still had to function. I had to pay the bills, take care of the kids, do all the things that a parent does. I had other elders who were still living, who were sick and needed care. I didn't have the luxury of taking that grieving break, although that would have been helpful—and healthier.

So, I worked for fourteen to sixteen hours straight, until I was ready to collapse from exhaustion. I remodeled every store. I redid all the displays. I decorated for every new sale. When the store closed and it was after hours, I would listen to music, sing, and cry while I designed. I didn't let it out all at once but in little bits at a time.

It took a good six months to cry out all my tears after my dad died, and, of course, in those six months somebody else died. I wasn't done; I was back at it again—but this time I knew how I processed it.

I never took time off, but work was my therapy. That was my drug of choice, and it was a very productive one. I just worked and cried in the privacy of my own space. When I was with customers, I had my public face on. I would greet them and be present and happy and help them find what they were looking for. I was able to take a small break from grieving in those moments, and that was a relief. I didn't have to grieve full time.

It wasn't until a couple years later, after my father and grand-parents had died, that I realized it took longer, maybe, for me to process because I only let little bits out at a time instead of having a total breakdown. I slid slowly into that rock bottom instead of diving headfirst.

THROUGH THE FOG

Grief looks different for everybody. Each person goes through the grief process in their own way and for different lengths of time. You might need six months of solid grieving, or a year, or you might let it out a little bit at a time like I did.

You could have advice from the best people on the planet, but until you're ready you can't move on. I have an older friend whose husband died, and she had to go through a two-year timeframe of dealing with her grief and adjusting to her loss. She calls this transitional time "the fog."

Grief and the ensuing fog can come for anyone, and you just need to give it time. If you move on too soon, you're not healed up and you can end up in a new broken situation, whether that's a bad relationship or battling an addiction. It's best not to make huge decisions until you get through the fog, so you don't make the wrong choices. If you do need to make a serious decision, make sure to consult an expert, get second and third opinions, and listen to your intuition.

You need to get through the fog in order to get to a healthier, happier place. You are not alone, and the fog will not last forever, that I can promise.

Know that there's a point when you're finished grieving, but that doesn't mean you will never grieve again. My dad died on Father's Day, so every year when Father's Day comes around,

I'm still melancholy. I choose to celebrate the magic memories I had with my dad and am grateful to be connected to all my cousins who are on his side of my family. Today, I have happy memories, and once in a while I shed a tear for those who have transitioned.

The pain of my loss has lessened with time; yet it had to be on *my* time. I've come to terms with my family's transition. Now, I feel my relatives who have passed are all spiritual beings helping me out here and there. I will often say to myself, "I wonder how my dad or grandparents would have dealt with this situation." Then I can almost hear their words of wisdom.

All their wisdom and memories are planted in the pocket of my heart, as an additional guide and resource for me, always. We are still very much connected; our relationship has just changed a little. I am always grateful for their memories and the legacy of wisdom they left for me.

Twenty years later, you still honor and grieve your loved ones in one way or another. It's not like they disappear from your heart. You just come to a different place where it's not as difficult as when it first happened.

Until you're ready and able to move on, nobody can push you. The door is open. There's no lock on the door, but you have to walk through it on your own.

SAY GOODBYE TO OTHER PEOPLE'S EXPECTATIONS

Just as there's no right or wrong length of time for the grieving process, there's also no right or wrong way to process that grief. When you're grieving and going through this personal situation, you're going to have a lot of people who try to help you through it—or expect you to just get over it.

How you grieve and process that grief is right for you. No one can tell you exactly what you need. Honor the time it takes for you to grieve. Walk and work through it rather than just trying to get over it.

Walking through the grieving journey is natural, normal, completely healthy, and sane. It's part of our process as human beings. Honor that part of you as much as you honor the part that laughs and plays and does fun things. That emotion of grief is just as good and helpful and purposeful as any other emotion we have.

It's sometimes looked down on in society or we're made to feel like we have to hide our grief. You can do whatever you choose to do with that, but don't hide it from yourself. It's like any kind of healing: if you want to heal, you're going to have to go through the pain. To get to that other side, you have to come to terms with it in your own way—and everybody has their own way of coming to terms with it. Some people may take time away from everybody else and pray or meditate in isolation. Others may choose to surround themselves with people or distract themselves in work or volunteering to take a break from the pain.

Too many people feel the "should" in a lot of parts of their lives. *I should feel this way.* Or *I should do this because I see other people grieving like this.* Find some way to honor what *you* need, whether that's taking a walk every night or going to bed early or just asking for help getting through the day. If you need to cry every night for six months, or journal, or take long walks, or hike, or do yoga every day to get through it—do *whatever* you need to do. It's all okay. There's no magic bullet to end your grief. There's no magic moment when you get over it; all grieving is individual.

There are also many ways to honor your loved one. You can have a memorial or ceremony personalized around the person who passed and those who remain. You can connect with others and share your favorite memories. Take pictures of them at different stages of their life, or of their house or whatever you want to remember about them, and make a collage with your favorite pictures. Do something so you have a memory and you honor that grieving time. You may even do things differently for different people that you lose. Just honor whatever comes to you, because honoring your loved one is part of healing. There's no right or wrong. However you need to heal is the best way.

I wouldn't worry that someone grieved too long or too hard. But I would be concerned if someone gets stuck in their grief, feeling like they've lost their identity and aren't sure how to continue forward in life. They may need more extensive help processing that grief.

And I would definitely be troubled by someone who isn't grieving the loss of a close loved one at all. If there's no crying, no feelings or emotions, they're not going through that process and something's not okay. They might be in denial, and that just means the grief will come out in some other way at another time. That person probably needs to get help from a therapist or trained professional.

Please check out the resource guide at the end of this book as well as my website for updated resources and additional activities that can point you toward the help you may need: www.SheilaMac.com/griefsupport.

WE'RE ALL MORTAL

Having a loved one pass can lead to questioning your own mortality and wondering how much time you have left. We're not promised anything beyond this moment. How do you want to live your life? What really matters?

Channel your grief into remembering to enjoy every moment of this space and this energy—your loved one would want you to do so. Don't wait for happiness; enjoy every single thing that you're given now. Create a gratitude practice. Make room for reading or prayers or meditation. Hang your favorite pictures, and make new memories. Give yourself a beautiful home environment full of positive, healing energy.

I have a sign out front of my house that reads, "Be happy. Always tell the truth. Work hard. Laugh out loud. Give thanks for your family. Say I love you. Laugh, giggle, be silly. See the world. Help others. Be grateful. Try new things. Say please and thank you. Dream big. Use kind words. Don't whine. Do your best. No running in the house. Be proud of yourself. And remember that you are loved."

This simple, admittedly cheesy sign brings a positive, joyful energy to my whole environment. People will stop and say, "I love that sign!" It makes their day. It makes me happy too, and then I'm spreading that to someone else.

As your grief passes, remember that you are in charge of your life. You get to choose happiness. You get to choose your environment because it affects every part of you. It affects your relationships, with children, with adults, with your pets. That energy affects how you show up at work. Do you have a beautiful place to rest? Can you make your bedroom a retreat? It doesn't have to cost a lot or be fancy or follow what the pages of a magazine show you. You don't have to go on vacation and spend thousands of dollars to sit outside and be grateful and meditate and do some yoga. You can create that space in your own life.

It can also be helpful to keep your routine during your time of grief. If you have an exercise routine, a work routine, a family routine, it's helpful to participate in those as much as you are able to. You need that healing space, but you also want to stay in society. You need that space between the grieving and the living, so you don't just get stuck in your grief.

Creating positive energy will attract more of that same energy. Then you're not just experiencing tragedy; you're turning your grief into the gift of a positive life shift.

LOVE CURES ALL

It's really important that you have support as you go through this time, but when your loved ones are all grieving too, it can bring up hurt feelings and other issues.

After a death, people tend to look at their connection to the loved one through the items that are left. They may fight over who gets what, but it's all just stuff. Don't let that fighting lead to the loss of another relationship. If you think about the wishes of your parent or the person who is transitioning on and leaving us, would they want to have their children fighting over stupid stuff? No, they would never want that. They want you to support each other through this difficult time.

I talked to a client last week who has four siblings. They just lost their parents, and they're trying to sell the family house. All five of them have to agree on the offer and sign off on the sale—but every time they get together, instead of saying "I love you" or sharing memories, all they do is fight. Eventually, they all stopped speaking to one another.

Each of them had a different reason for why they did or did not want to get rid of the house. One person was tied to a memory. Somebody else was ready to sell it because they didn't want to think about the house without their mom, because it hurt. They wanted to get away as quickly as possible. Another one needed to sit and process it and have time to say goodbye.

I talked with them and suggested that they think about what their mom would want. How would she feel knowing that she left something that's only causing everybody to be upset? That's not honoring her memory. The cost of maintaining that house, paying for upkeep and property taxes and insurance, is not worth squabbling over—to say nothing of the cost of those precious familial relationships.

Eventually, they came to an agreement to just honor their mother and thank her memory. They sold the house right away, split it up the way she desired, and were done with it. And now they meet every Sunday morning for brunch, just like they used to when their parents were alive. They honor their mother through loving one another.

Love cures all. Love is a healer, and that's what helps people out of the hole that a death leaves.

HOW TO HELP OTHERS

If you're reading this to help somebody else get through their grief, that is a kind instinct, but you also want to allow and honor their space. How can we be there for other people and support them but honor the space, time, and process that they need to go through as they grieve?

Start by asking permission. You may want to bring something over, or show them some love with a card, a dinner, or an offer to take them out. Ask if that's okay—and give them the opportunity to decline. The most important thing is to honor their space in that and ask, "How are you doing? If you want to talk about it, I'm available. If you just want to talk about other things and have space, I get it. You let me know. I'm here as much or as little as you need me to be."

There are lots of ways to help someone who is grieving. You can offer to pick up the phone and call them when they're available. You can offer to come over and talk or be available in a crisis. If they want to escape what they're going through a little bit, you can take them to see a movie or get a pedicure or anything that will distract them from thinking about their loss for a short while.

That gives them the choice. As we've established, people sometimes need that breathing space between grieving and not wanting to talk about it anymore. Or they don't want to get buried under that emotion, so they need their friends to pull them out. They may just need a girls' night out where their problems don't exist, just for those few hours. They'll grieve in their own time. They just need you to help give them that break from grieving.

Other times you need that friend who will stay up all night with you and let you cry your eyes out, listening to you and not really saying much, just being there and being present.

Either way, always ask permission so you're honoring that person's personal grief process. You're there for them but offering what they need and want rather than trying to make their grief look different.

GRIEVING THE LOSS OF YOUR IDENTITY AS A MOTHER

The grief process goes to another level when a parent loses a child, whether it's a miscarriage or a child who was in your life for a long time. This is a deeper pain than most people can imagine or will ever experience. It is the most difficult experience a woman can go through.

Again, you're going to need your own timeline, to be able to honor all these stages of grief and know that you're honoring that memory and doing whatever you need to heal. It doesn't matter what anybody else says. Some people won't understand how personal that experience is. If they haven't been through it, they just won't get it.

This type of healing is a sacred process and so individual and unique that nobody, no matter what, can tell you how it has to go. You just have to honor your own way.

Finding out you can't get pregnant or have children is a form of grief, too. You have to let go of this idea of motherhood. There are obviously different ways to be a mother, but it's grieving that possibility of becoming pregnant and giving birth to a child.

Sometimes you can find a soul purpose through this loss. It may be an adoption. It may be some other form of a family. It might be helping somebody else's child in some way. If somebody is holding space for a child to come into their life, one way or another, physically or through some other means, that is going to show up in its own beautiful way. Whatever the form of the child, or the purpose of mothering or fathering, will show up in the way it's supposed to.

I was told after my first child that it would be completely impossible to have any more children. It was over.

At first, I blamed myself. *Why did this happen to me? Did I eat the wrong foods?* Then I was angry—at myself and at the doctors. It was so disheartening to watch the big family I'd always imagined disappear. I didn't want my son to be an only child like I was. I'd always pictured brothers and sisters.

I had to feel that sorrow and grieve that loss. But then I found new hope. I had been in the foster care system for a little while when I was younger, so I chose to help other kids who were in that situation. I decided to foster to adopt.

Three other children joined our family—and they were a beautiful fit. Then, at the end of that journey of adoption, I found out I was pregnant. "How did this happen??" I asked my gynecologist.

The doctor said, "You don't know how pregnancy happens?"

It had been eight years, and I'd been told it would never happen, not in a million years.

Maybe in the spiritual realm those children were in the family for the length of time they needed to be in the family, and it's almost like it was destined. We were called to fill that space. And then two more children showed up, back-to-back, my daughter and my youngest son. As soon as I saw them, it was like, "Well, there you are!"

But before that, it was like I didn't get to meet them yet because I had to serve these other children. Somehow, out there in the universe, there was this plan that was beyond us. We needed to parent, and my first son needed to be the brother, and all those children needed to be in the family. I was supposed to have each and every one of those beautiful children in my life, however they showed up.

If you or somebody you love is going through those situations, and if they're open to ways to share love and to serve and it's coming from love in all its forms, whatever is right shows up. It all lines up.

What are you guided to do? Maybe it's helping with other children or volunteering as a backup foster parent. That might prepare you for having your own children while giving these other children love that they don't have from anyone else in their life.

FROM GRIEF TO GRATITUDE

We feel grief for the death of a loved one, but we can also feel grief for the loss of a lifestyle or mourn a relationship. There can be a time of grief for losing a relationship, losing a job, losing a house, losing anything that was a part of you and now isn't anymore. These are big life shifts, and it makes sense to honor them as you move on.

You have to go through this process of grieving them before you move on and see the benefits of whatever that change is. When you do, you usually see that ultimately it works out for the best.

For me, I've moved many times. I've had many different jobs. I've made many shifts based on the seasons of my life. With every house I move from and every shift I make—even if I know I'm leveling up—I say goodbye and give gratitude to that time of my life. I thank the memories and send love as I move on. It's not an official ceremony, but it's something I've always done to mark these shifts, and it can take some of the sting out of a big change.

Whether someone dies or you're going through a breakup or you just felt like you didn't get closure when you were laid off from a job, create a ceremony to help you through the healing process. Write a letter to the person who left, acknowledging your sadness, anger, or loneliness. Say anything you wish you had said while they were still here. Then send off your memories with love. Be thankful for the good parts and acknowledge that these things happen, and now you're going your separate ways. You'll have that release because it's such a healing place to come from gratitude. That energy is felt, and it will send you better and better places.

Then, when you've moved into your new place or at your new job or in a new relationship, you will be grateful for the clean start that lets you make it as beautiful and fun and perfect for your lifestyle right now as possible.

APPLYING THE BOOTS FORMULA TO GRIEF
BEING

My relatives passed away within a short period of time, but I still had family who were living; I had relatives in the hospital. Some of them also knew they didn't have a lot of time left, so for their sake, as well as my own, I had to make sure that I showed up for them not in a place of grieving.

I also had to decide how to show up for my children, my clients, and for myself.

Taking a break from grieving while I was at work served me because it honored my need for that space. I made the decision of how I was going to show up for work. I told Laurie, my sales manager at the stores, "When I come into work, I take that piece of me that is grieving, and I put it down so I can serve my clients." That was my choice, and it felt like literally setting down a weight to take that break. Then I could pick it back up when I had private moments. At home, I would journal to let everything out.

I made the decision to show up for myself and everyone else in a certain way. I stayed on my schedule and followed my routine—and that saved me. It let me smile and laugh even though I had lost somebody a few days ago. I didn't get stuck in that grieving place. I didn't get dragged down into a full-time depression or extended period of low energy that pulls down other parts of life.

ORIENTATION

The Orientation part of this process was knowing, "This is where I am." This is what happened. It is what it is, and it's something we couldn't change. We did the best we could—we tried every surgery, alternative treatments, and extra care. We did everything we could and, sometimes, this is just the way it is.

ORDER OF OPERATIONS

Because I'm an only child, I unfortunately had the duty of organizing my relatives' funerals and closing out their affairs. Some had wills, some had trusts, and others didn't have much at all. I had to figure out how to make the arrangements—and how to pay for them all. That is a big responsibility for anyone, but it was even more difficult at such a young age. I was going through something emotional, I was grieving, and I had to just set that aside as best I could and make the decisions: Do they want to be buried this way or that way? What about this religion, that practice? How do I honor the family?

I didn't *want* to think about any of that. What if I made the wrong decision? I saw relatives I hadn't seen in years, and I just wanted to make sure that any family drama was set aside in order to honor this person's passing.

THINKING

Sometimes, we need to create some space between grieving and living so we don't just get stuck in our grief. There's a balance, a dance between the part of yourself that wants to go out with your friends and be with people and talk about other things and the part of yourself that goes over and over the story of your loss.

It's healing to move on, when you're ready to do so. You still love the person you lost, and you still honor their memory, but you need to go on—for all the other people in your life and for yourself. It really helped me to acknowledge the person who passed away and to ask myself, "What would they want for me? What would be their highest wish for me?"

My loved ones would want me to be happy while I'm here, not stuck in grieving. That was when I realized that not grieving all the time actually honors their memory even more. I would never want my children to sit and grieve and wallow for years and years. I would want them to heal. I'd understand that they had grieved, but I'd want to see them have happy moments, to live their lives and enjoy everything here and to do everything they want for themselves.

STEPPING UP

What I went through, and with other people that I've worked with on grief, I've learned the healing timeframe and process is unique to each individual.

Stepping up means stepping into your rituals, routines, the things you know will help you. The only person who's going to write a prescription for grieving is you. You're the only person who will know if you need to go do yoga or hike in the hills or write or paint. Whatever it is, you'll almost naturally go to. You'll know, and it'll be therapeutic. That's what's going to help you the most.

FROM GRIEVING ROCK BOTTOM TO MOMENT OF EMPOWERMENT

My grandmother was the last of my grandparents to pass away. I had to clean out her house, sell her furniture, and give away or donate everything else. There was nothing particularly valuable, but it had value to me because of our memories. We'd grown very close during the long time I took care of her.

For the first six months following her death, all I could do was go to her home and look at everything. It was hard for me to touch anything, and I certainly didn't want somebody else to go through Grandma's stuff. I loved Grandma; I couldn't do that to her things. I was really conflicted, but I just needed that time to process. I would go there after work for an hour and just sit there, looking at everything and remembering who she was and how much she meant to me.

Then, one day, I was ready.

I called Goodwill and let go of all of it. It was cathartic—I had my time, I did my grieving, I walked through that tunnel and got to the other side, and I was ready to release it. I didn't feel guilty or bad or need to explain it. I honored her and did what I needed to do.

Re-BOOT Activity: How to Honor Yourself during the Grief Process

Everyone grieves differently, and a person goes through the stages of grief whether they have lost a loved one, their family, a friend, a pet who is family, or even when going from one stage of life or from rock bottom back into action. Grieving is a part of the healing and reorganizing process.

Honor your need to grieve. You matter, you are loved, and grieving is the best gift you can give yourself. Don't pretend everything is okay; give yourself the gift of space and time for grieving.

Here's a checklist of what that may look like. Check off the boxes of the actions that you think may help you the most. Then refer back to your list when you need help processing your grief.

Create a buddy system of family and friends.

If you are the one responsible for making final arrangements, or if you need to seek legal advice, it is important to have other people you trust and who you can turn to for help. This is the most difficult time to make centered, thoughtful decisions, because you just want to have that time to grieve. There are also people who may try to take advantage of someone who has experienced a loss.

If at all possible, get a friend, family member, or legal advisor to help you before signing contracts or making costly commitments on arrangements. If needed, write everything down and go to lunch or meditate on the arrangements overnight before making a final commitment. Review any will or trust to see if your loved one has already paid for or designed a final ceremony. Legal fees and extra taxes could surprise you. It may be wise to check with a local attorney or your loved one's accountant or a trusted CPA to help guide you on these matters.

Take care of your health.

Check in with your regular doctor, and ask a friend to help you with accountability on your wellness routine. Taking time out to rest, eat healthy foods, and exercise can help you maintain a state of peace and wellness even through this grieving time. Being in your best health honors your loved one's life and memory.

Find a way to honor your loved one's life while you live yours to the fullest.

It takes effort to live in the present and not dwell on the past. Grieving can take months or years. The relationship with your loved one changes to that of loving memories, but you can find ways to honor the person who has passed.

One thing that helped me was getting involved in programs that helped others dealing with the health issues my dad and one of my grandparents had. I contributed to a Race for the Cure marathon and other cancer research programs in memory of my father. I was also involved in a dementia fundraiser, in memory of my grandfather.

I also thought about what my family members who had passed would truly want for me. I could almost hear them telling me to live a good life, help others, and always do my best. As I move forward with my life, I know that I am still honoring their memory and legacy.

Postpone major life changes at this time.

People often attempt a life shift or adjustment to heal the pain and then regret the decision when they are finally out of the fog again. Try to hold off on making any major changes, such as moving, remarrying, changing jobs, or having another child.

Be patient with beautiful, authentic *you*.

It can take months or even years to heal from a major loss and accept your changed life. Although you will continue to make steps forward, there will still be days and moments where emotions show up. These emotions are part of the healing process; they are normal, and they are okay. Send love to the memories of your loved ones and to yourself.

Seek outside help when necessary.

If your grief is affecting your day-to-day life, if it becomes too much to bear, or if it is overwhelming, seek professional assistance to help work through this time. Asking for help is a sign of strength; we all need help from time to time.

Seek out your most loving peer group.

Talk about your feelings to relatives and friends you can trust. Get plugged into support groups for your specific loss. This connection to a group of people who are experienced in dealing with the loss of a loved one, and who have walked in your shoes, can help you heal and readjust to your loved one's transition. In most cases, close family and friends will all be grieving a little bit differently, so getting additional support and connection will help everyone involved.

I created the B & B Community online as a way to connect people who may be going through a grieving experience and would otherwise feel alone. There is power in numbers, and you can join us at https://www.facebook.com/groups/SheilaMacShowBandB/about/.

How to Help Others Grieve

If someone you care about has lost a loved one, there are many ways you can help them through the grieving process.

Give space to the art of loving listening.

Create time to have coffee, go for a walk, or just talk and encourage them to share their feelings and memories. Sometimes just being a listening ear can be a relief for your friend or loved one.

Don't offer advice, just love and listen.

It doesn't help the grieving person when you say, "You'll get over it in time." The gift of being present in their moment of grieving is all they need.

Step up where you can.

This can include anything that gives your friend or loved one space to grieve: babysitting, sharing your talents such as helping with a gathering, sending out messages for your grieving friend, or creating a team of their trusted friends to help with cooking and running errands while they tend to their other loved ones.

Be patient.

Remember that it can take a long time to recover from a major loss. Make yourself available, but if they don't want to talk, that is okay too. There will be times when your friend may prefer space, so you can help with a loving check-in and reminder that you're there for them if they need a friend to talk to or just to go do something silly or different and not discuss the loss at all. Even in serious grieving, a person may ask for just a night out to not think about it all and not grieve. That is okay and often part of the process as well.

Encourage professional help when necessary.

Don't hesitate to recommend professional help when you feel someone is experiencing too much pain to cope alone. Signs may include not getting back to work, stopping a healthy eating and exercise routine, poor hygiene, or using drugs or alcohol to cope. If you see any of these symptoms, it may be time to connect them with more support.

For further resources for grief, I have a resource section in this book, and the most current updates can be found on my website. My goal is to make sure that as you heal on your terms, you can connect to as many resources as possible. I will also be adding additional activities that may help you get through the grieving process at www.SheilaMac.com/griefsupport.

🎁 *My Gift to You* 🎁

Walk out through the 7 Stages of Grief toward healing.

The seven stages of grieving are REAL and a natural part of healing and coming to terms with the loss of a loved one. If you are going through the grieving process.

I have created a free gift for you: Get a 7-week email program to help you recognize, embrace, and learn to cope with the 7 Stages of Grief. Learn the strategies to honor this process and new ways to celebrate the memories of your loved one.

- Shock and denial—You will probably react to learning of the loss with numbing disbelief.
- Pain and guilt
- Anger and bargaining
- "Depression," reflection, loneliness
- The upward turn
- Reconstruction and working through
- Acceptance and hope

Go to www.sheilamacshow.com/grieving.

CHAPTER 3

SHIFT OR GET OFF THE POT (RELATIONSHIPS)

Angela is a friend and client in her late forties who hit rock bottom while going through a divorce.

Angela's artistic talent is a big part of her essence, a way for her to express her emotions, her truth, her love, but Angela's husband didn't like her to talk about her art, let alone create art in the house. He is a very militant and structured man, and she is the creative artist type. When Angela and her husband were dating and newlyweds, they had fun. She felt free to express herself.

That sense of freedom withered away after they had children. Angela's husband expected the household to be run with a certain structure and the children to be raised in a strict way of life. Angela wanted to share her passion for art with her kids, making murals and crafting handmade ornaments for the holidays. Her husband didn't think that was necessary and hated coming home to a messy house—even yelling and putting her down in front of the children if he felt they had gone overboard with art projects.

They fought often over the years. The children loved doing art projects with their mother when they were younger, able to express the artistic parts of themselves. As they got older, however, they saw less of who she really was; instead, Angela's children saw somebody living in conflict with herself. They saw her get in trouble when she made her art, so they kept their passions and talents locked in a box, too.

When I asked Angela about her happiest moments, she said it was when she and her children were decorating those ornaments, making gifts for everybody. Even little Sam, who wasn't great at art projects, used his computer programming skills to create his own style of art. They put their heart into their gifts for grandparents, aunts, and uncles. When their father came home, he said, "That's stupid. Just buy them a gift—we've got money."

Angela felt like she was holding her breath in every aspect of her life and not expressing her true self. She worked in a professional, noncreative field. Her husband expected a strict, disciplined household. Angela's artistic side was suffocating. Family, friends, even therapists pointed out how restrictive Angela's lifestyle had become. Nobody was happy in that house—not even the dog.

For about ten years, Angela did everything possible to stay in her marriage for her children. She and her husband ended up sleeping in separate rooms and leading separate lives in the same house, prolonging the pain of growing apart. Leaving seemed an obvious choice but nobody could take that step for Angela. There isn't a human being on the planet who could have helped her walk through that door—until she was finally ready, which happened, unfortunately, only after she got very sick and ended up in the hospital.

There, Angela realized that if she didn't stop the stress and get away from this continuous torture eating her up inside, she might literally die. Finally, she reached out and was able to say, "I'm ready to do this because I don't have any other choice."

Lying in the hospital bed was her rock-bottom moment—but that's not to say her situation couldn't get any harder. The circle of people they most related to as a family did not support Angela and her children through the divorce because they come from a very traditional, religious background where divorce is not considered an option. Her children were cut off from one set of grandparents. Angela lost friends from her place of worship. People she worked with were pissed off at her.

Staying was costing Angela her health. She made her choice and stepped into it—but at what cost?

SHOULD I STAY OR SHOULD I GO?

We'll look at how Angela continued walking through and out of her rock-bottom moment later in this chapter. For now, though, let's focus on the fact that she found herself in a situation familiar to many women: deciding whether to stay in a relationship or leave.

For this chapter, we're looking at a breakup as a rock bottom—but it's not the only way a relationship can end or be redefined. There is a spectrum along which every relationship falls, and the true rock-bottom moment comes when you have to decide whether you've outgrown a marriage or if you're going to recommit to it.

Sometimes, as with the death of a spouse, that choice is taken away from you. (If the sudden change in your relationship is a death, you can refer to chapter 7, which is about grief. That shift is outside of your control, and you'll want to approach it from a different perspective.) Other times, as with abusive situations, the choice may be obvious—but very difficult to make. We'll discuss abuse in greater depth in the next chapter.

Whatever state your relationship is in, you can own your role in it, which allows you to take back your power and own your happiness as well.

So, the first step is to ask yourself, "Can we make it work?"

If you really want to make it work, and both parties are all-in for that, then that's the goal. That's great!

Of course, there are also relationships that are never going to be healed, and not moving on from those just prolongs the pain of ripping off that Band-Aid. At a certain point, you're hurting everybody. You all realize it's not working out. The kids know. Everybody knows. It's like being in hell.

If you're stuck half-in and half-out of a relationship, you won't be able to pull out of your rock-bottom moment. You may be so focused on the possible end of your relationship that you're not showing up at work as much or you're not able to be present with your children.

It's really important to get to a place where you're taking your power back. There are beautiful ways to help heal a relationship. But if it isn't going to work, know that ending the relationship isn't going to take your happiness away.

The most loving, effective way possible to move on—whether that's to repair the relationship or make as clean a break as possible—is to own your part of the responsibility and go forward. There are two people here. No matter what has happened in the past, it's not your fault nor the other party's fault 100 percent. Both partners are responsible for some part of how you got to this point. Taking responsibility for your part empowers you to choose what your relationship is going to look like in the future.

When you're able to pull from the relationship all the gifts that empower you to make different choices—whether it's good memories or knowing that you're not settling—you can be thankful for the life lessons learned. You know that you are not a victim—you are powerful. Once you make a choice and take that decisive action, you are honoring yourself.

In this chapter, we'll look at making the choice to walk away from a relationship as well as what it looks like if you choose to reconnect.

GROWING APART

At some point, you may realize that you and your partner have grown apart and reconnection isn't just going to happen by magic. You may have gone to a therapist, sought religious counseling, or seen a life coach, but nothing changes, and agreements continue to be broken. There's a point where you agree that if it doesn't work, you need to honor what you've had and move on. You can make a conscious choice not to keep trying to reconnect.

I got married young—to the boyfriend I told you about in the Introduction, the father of my son (and all my children). We got married for the wrong reasons, with a lot of pressure from relatives. We couldn't agree on anything other than how we raised our kids. That was our one aligning factor, but we had nothing else in common, so we fought about our different visions, values, and directions for our lives. It was a constant struggle.

I stayed in the relationship desperately attempting to do the "right thing," yet we are both so incredibly different that we had little in common. We mostly did whatever he liked doing for fun, and I set aside all my passions. It was a huge expense on my soul. No one was happy because we had different ideas of what our life was supposed to look like, and the children felt this as well. It wasn't that there was no love; it was just that we weren't compatible in our life purposes.

Ultimately, the best decision was for us not to be in that marriage anymore because it wasn't working for either of us. Once our children were grown, we agreed to go on our own separate paths.

Before you make that final decision, it may be a good idea to have a ninety-day period where you just put in one more shot, if that's what you want and both people agree. During that time, you and your significant other date each other again, and you can use that time to really try to renew your love for that person.

Here are some ideas for things to try during those ninety days (feel free to customize them to fit your situation):

- Spend time doing things together as a couple. Take your lover out for a movie or favorite dining experience.
- Dress up the way you used to when you first dated and create fun, spontaneous things to do, like you both used to really enjoy.
- Find a babysitter or puppy sitter and take a mini vacation away together.
- Create a romantic bedroom at home if travel is not in the budget. Dim the lights, dress up in something sexy or nothing at all, give your mate a hot-oil massage, and get as loud and passionate as you did when you were young lovers.
- Write love notes or send romantic or steamy text messages to your loved one.
- Have an adult ditch day: take an afternoon off from work while the kids are at school and invite your spouse to do the same. Time for adult play!

Don't discuss the issues or the disagreements during this time, just focus on the love as much as possible.

Then, if things still don't change, you've set that date and now you're honoring your own agreements to yourself.

Each person has a responsibility to themselves to honor their own standards and needs. You're going to have to set that boundary and, at a certain point, you're going to have to follow through on the decision you've made.

If you decide to leave, you can't keep threatening your spouse hoping they'll change. Nope, this is it. You've had the talk, and you're done. It's been however many years—plus ninety days—and it's hurting both of you, so you agree to stop. You gave it one last try, and now you can move forward in a loving way to move apart because you're not aligned anymore.

INFIDELITY

But what happens when that period of growing apart leads to one or both partners choosing to be unfaithful?

The stability of a marriage or relationship is often threatened by outside situations. You don't have enough time together because you need to care for your sick mom or your kid's going through adolescent angst and needs your support. There's a season in life and in relationships where those interruptions are going to be your normal.

Unfortunately, that season is when people may seek connection with someone outside the marriage and have an affair, emotionally or physically.

Affairs tend to happen slowly and gradually—and it's not because two people don't love each other. It's not always intentional or done out of hatred. Those people want a certain level of connection in a relationship, and when that connection is disrupted—even for a reason that makes perfect sense when you look at it objectively—they may look for it elsewhere.

Infidelity is gut-wrenching and painful. When you are in a committed relationship and the other person cheats, you may feel like it's a judgment against you or a blow to your confidence. *Am I not pretty or handsome enough? Did I not do enough?*

Having an emotional connection with somebody outside of the relationship may not be cheating in the traditional definition of infidelity, but it feels the same to the person who finds out about the affair. In fact, physical affairs often mean less than emotional ones.

Learning about your partner's infidelity comes as a shock because you probably thought you were happy. Even if the other person doesn't decide to leave, finding out that your partner had an affair can shake up your relationship—and your whole life.

When faced with an infidelity, you have to make the personal choice of whether to stay or to leave. Some people can get back together, work it out, and start fresh—and they do great. Others may decide not to take the chance of going through this rock bottom again.

You cannot change another human being; you can't control them. They're going to do whatever they're going to do. That person chose to dishonor your commitment, and that's on their integrity. You may not even be able to control whether they stay or go. But there are two people in this relationship, and you *can* control yourself and what you do next.

Self-love is really important, as is honoring yourself and not jumping into the victim role. You can decide who you want to have in your life and what happens if someone crosses the line that you set. You have to know what that no-deal point is for you. It's an individual decision; there's no judgment about where you choose to draw that line.

Your body will tell you. Your emotions will tell you. You may feel resentful or hurt, and something will feel very off to you. When this first happens, you may not be able to put your finger on it; it just doesn't feel like the relationship is aligned. You may get a feeling in the pit of your stomach or an ache for no reason.

Even more important is that you realize that you are empowered to know where that line is—and that the door is open. You're not locked in a cage; you have the freedom to walk away.

If you can't feel the same with this person as you did earlier in the relationship, when you were happy, you'll know that it's not going to work. You may still love them, but you have to love yourself enough to know that you can't forgive their behavior, and you don't have to be a part of it. It's not worth staying in a relationship that doesn't work just to have somebody in your life.

You deserve to be in a relationship with honesty and integrity. Surround yourself with people who are aligned with your values. Take responsibility for and control of your life, and you'll take back your power.

SET THEM FREE—AND YOU SET YOURSELF FREE, TOO

There's a beautiful ceremony you can do when you are finally disconnected from a relationship that didn't work. You can send love and release them. Write a letter that says everything you feel, and then burn it or send it off in a balloon.

That allows you to set free that whole relationship and send gratitude for the lesson. Now you know what you *don't* want in your life. You honor and love the good parts you did see in your former partner. Obviously to have a relationship, you had to see something at some point that was a light, good part. Then you release them—and you release yourself at the same time.

When you do that, it frees you up and gives you the space to have people who are a better fit for you show up in your life. You're not still stuck in that old story. You've set it free, given it love, and let it go. If there's a better fit who's more aligned with who you are and your values and your vision for life, those people will show up. Then you don't get stuck on the old story of why that person was bad; you take responsibility and release them.

Whether or not they gave you closure, you took your own and gave it to them in return. Then you can move on in peace, whether you're going through a breakup or divorce or temporary disconnect in a relationship.

REIGNITING YOUR LOVE

What happens when you choose to stay instead of go?

Perhaps you've been so focused on working and parenting for so long that you've just fallen into those roles and neglected your roles as partners. Then, when you retire or your kids move out or another shift occurs, all of a sudden you're living with a stranger. You have to figure out how to reconnect with this person at the level of a partner, not as a parent or somebody else working to support the household.

You can work together as a team again. You can rebuild your connection and give yourselves permission to be a young, married couple again—even if you're older.

RECOMMITMENT CONTRACT

From what I've seen in my own relationships and seeing the ups and downs my friends and clients have gone through, you have your relationship and then you have outside factors, which are important to identify. Maybe you have to go to holiday dinners with your in-laws who belittle you. Maybe you have financial issues that are causing stress.

Once you've had children, in particular, life feels different. You have to do chores and help with homework. You have to pay for their expenses and discipline them when something goes wrong. You may be working more hours away from your family—even though it's all done out of love. This isn't a completely mis-aligned relationship; the passionate times are just diminishing because you're busy doing something that may be important for the survival of the family.

You can't change some of those factors—but some of them you can. How can you change what you can? How are you going to respond differently so it doesn't affect your couple unit or your family unit, so that it's not going to be a problem anymore? That has nothing to do with your love, and as a couple you can own that and decide what you can do proactively to make adjustments.

Think about writing a recommitment contract. Part of your contract may include how many date nights per week you want, or how you're going to celebrate holidays. You may strategize what you'll do if something happens—if the kids need something or your mom gets sick or your boss makes you work long hours on a deadline. You have a preplanned understanding of how to continue honoring each other in those situations. (You'll also find an activity at the end of this chapter that walks you through how to create a relationship agreement.)

You're going to have fun, reunite, and do crazy, wild things like we all did when we were younger. Who the hell cares? You're not worried about other people's opinions. You're just going to do whatever romantic things you did when you were in your twenties or thirties, so you can rekindle that relationship.

Maybe you want to go on a second honeymoon. You may decide to renew your vows, especially if you want to change your commitments or reacknowledge what you're honoring in each other.

If there was infidelity, you may want to start over, dating again, and then make a new commitment, contract, or vow with one another. You don't have to make it formal and invite people to a party. You can just say it to one another in your backyard or on a trip. You can have a beautiful moment where you recommit to your fresh start, to moving forward, and to your wonderful new relationship.

If there's an ability to have open conversations and to connect back and see that it's not really about loving each other, it's about all this outside stuff, you can work around that and still have that time to continue in this beautiful relationship that you both want to maintain.

COMMUNICATION

As we all know, men and women are different. That difference is really clear in how women and men communicate.

Men are direct. They often say what they mean and mean what they say. Rarely is there hidden meaning. If they say, "I'm going to be late," it's because they're going to be late—not because they want to make a point or don't love you. When they talk to each other, they say things like, "Hey buddy, you gained thirty pounds. What are you going to do about it?" That doesn't mean "you're ugly;" that's just how they talk.

Women wouldn't say that—even if it's true—because in general we tend to be more emotional. We don't like to point out our flaws.

You want to have an awareness of the difference in how women and men communicate so you can learn the other person's language and learn how to be direct.

You may choose to have a word to use if you start to go back to the old patterns established before you recommitted to this relationship. If you start to fight over the toilet paper roll or something stupid like that, what crazy code word can you use—something completely silly—that will break that moment and remind you of your real love?

When you're playful and laughing, you're not going to go to

that negative place. When it's something more serious, you may need to communicate beyond that one word. Maybe you have to say, "When you were late and I had made dinner, but you didn't call, I felt neglected." Or, "Hey, I'm drowning over here. I need to talk about this as soon as possible."

From a woman's standpoint, having an agreed-upon word or direct statement is going to reach home to a man a lot more than deciding to show him—because he may never see it. It may go over his head. He wants to know what you need, so he can provide it.

USE YOUR LOVE LANGUAGES

I have five boys and one daughter, so I've learned how to communicate with the boys—and that's really blessed me for other relationships. I realize I just need to be direct.

I highly recommend the book *The Five Love Languages* by Gary Chapman to learn about the other person's love language. This book says that each person expresses love and responds best through using one of five ways of communicating, or what they call our love languages: words of affirmation, acts of service, receiving gifts, quality time, and physical touch.

All six of my children have completely different love languages. My youngest son's is physical touch; he's always been a hugger. When I text him, I say, "I'm sending you a big hug!" He'll text back, "I caught it! I'm sending one back."

My daughter is not a hugger; her love language is quality time. She'll come over for slumber parties where we stay up talking until the sun rises the next day.

It's good to know your significant other's temperament and the love language that aligns with that. We all have different languages, so try to talk and text in the love language that means the most to your partner, because then they feel loved. If it's gifts, then get something small or inexpensive. Maybe they love to do sports and it's a priority for them to work out often. That doesn't mean they're taking time away from you; that's just who they are. They're not going to change. That's a beautiful part of them. But when you understand it, you can work around it.

Encourage your partner to speak your language, too. If you need alone time or a break to go get a manicure, ask for it. That's the biggest gift for someone who needs quiet time—and by asking for it, your partner isn't wondering, "Why doesn't she want to talk to me?"

Once you both understand your temperaments and advanced needs, you can be successful in your relationship—while still being true to who each of you are.

APPLYING THE BOOTS FORMULA TO RELATIONSHIPS

You can use the BOOTS Formula to help you move into whatever choice you've made for your relationship.

BEING

Who are you Being? Who are you showing up as at work and all the other places you go, versus who do you show up as with the other person in this relationship? Is how you're showing up with that person aligned with how you feel about him?

There are two people in a relationship. You may have grown

apart, whatever the reason. That doesn't matter as much as owning your personal responsibility.

If you have children, it's important to note that you are their relationship example. You're modeling how to deal with a relationship breaking up, even a divorce, how to grieve, or how to rekindle a relationship. Later on, that will empower your children—or other loved ones, like younger brothers and sisters—to deal with a similar situation, should they find themselves faced with one.

It's not so much what you say and teach, it's what you actually *do* that will help empower the other people in your life to get through their own crises in the future. You want your child to watch you and think, "Oh, so that's how I deal with that if it ever happens in my life, the way my mom dealt with it. That's the way I'm going to do it because she owned it. She took care of it, and she did her best, so that's what I'm going to do, too."

ORIENTATION

Your Orientation is that it's not better than it is, it's not worse; it is where it is. But you have to put yourself in there. You're honoring yourself and your promise to now move out of this relationship or stay in it and make it stronger. But you need to be responsible for the role you played in it.

Who were you Being? If you're able to answer that question honestly, you're not beating yourself up; you're gaining awareness that maybe you've changed. Maybe the other person has, and they have different values or they're just not a healthy person for you to be around now. It's still your responsibility to assess whatever you contributed to that so that you're able to move forward as a really solid, whole person.

Unless you take that personal responsibility, your emotions or circumstances are going to control how you choose to show up every day. Then who's in control of your life?

But the minute you own it, then guess what? Now you're in charge.

ORDER OF OPERATIONS

The decision you make about where to take your relationship will determine your Order of Operations. What do you need to do if you stay? What needs to happen for you to go?

Either way, how can you live the best life with the person with whom you have the most important relationship: yourself?

Doing this work now will allow you to re-attract your current partner or attract a new relationship later, if that's right for you. Most people don't want to jump right into the next relationship the day after they get divorced. But when you're ready, open, and aligned with that possibility, you're not going to repeat your patterns and end up with the same person as your previous partner, just in a different body, doing that same dance. This self-analysis step allows you to make that shift—even if your partner absolutely won't change.

THINKING

Time goes by quickly, and if your relationship ends you may think those five or ten years were ruined, but blaming the other person or the situation makes you the victim. It takes away your power.

You can choose to be in control and not let that affect you.

You get better outcomes just from that choice. When you're in control, you can choose to show up differently. You can walk away. You get to choose how to react.

STEPPING UP

Whatever choice you make, you have to step up into that decision.

You are going to get pushback from other people who want you to live on their terms, whether it's a religion, family, or friends. That's a huge part of whatever decision you make. You may redesign your relationship in a way that's different or non-traditional. Even if you're staying, it may be a very different look—and that's okay.

FROM RELATIONSHIP ROCK BOTTOM TO MOMENT OF EMPOWERMENT

Angela's moment of empowerment came when she decided to walk through the door and get a divorce, even though that was exactly what she had fought so hard *not* to do.

She took back her power by realizing that she was not a victim. Even when she made the announcement in the hospital and people stopped visiting, she had to be really strong. First, she had to recover. Then she had to get an attorney and figure out all the steps that people—particularly couples with children—have to go through to dissolve their legal union.

The blessing for them is that they love their kids. Even though their concepts of how to raise them and show their love are very different, that love is real. Angela and her now-ex-husband were able to come to a fair agreement because they put their children's needs ahead of their own. That was a beautiful thing, and it was helpful for Angela as she moved through this life shift.

She asked, "Who am I going to be through this?" Angela was healing, recovering, and having to face a lot of rejection—but she was also being a strong mom in the face of challenges. She knew it would be a lonely tunnel, but she also knew that she didn't have any other option other than to go through it.

Next, she had to ask, "Where am I?" Damn, I'm in the hospital, losing money, and I'm probably going to have to file for unemployment, if not bankruptcy.

Then, she asked, "What do I do first, second, and third?" She had to understand what steps to take. She had to get legal advice, working with somebody to help her get through the divorce itself. Going against the grain can feel very lonely, so we found some people outside the situation for her to connect with for support.

Angela had to reorganize her finances because there's a cost that comes with being willing to step away from some of the comfort—even though it ultimately wasn't comfortable to live in that kind of situation. She had to understand that, and then she had to go on COBRA health insurance because she wasn't able to work.

Once she got back on her feet, Angela had to go get her own place. She didn't feel like she was physically capable of living in her old house, so they sold it and she got her own space.

The fourth step was to ask, "How can I create a better life for myself and my children?" Angela had to create a vision of what she wanted her life to look like.

Finally, Angela completed the BOOTS Formula by Stepping Up into her vision for her new life. She's now gone into a different field, one where she can express her art, and she teaches part time at a small private school that has an art program.

Angela is so much happier, because she just needed to be herself. Her kids are happier, too. They don't have to deal with the pressure in a house filled with conflict. They can just be with their mom and see who she really is. Their dad gives them structure, and they love him, too. There's something really beautiful about getting to know and appreciate all the parts of yourself.

Ultimately, Angela had to be strong enough to realize what she wants for herself and her children—and then model that. She wants them to be strong people, with boundaries that need to be aligned with who they are. She wants them to be able to have a happy relationship someday, and she doesn't want them to give themselves up or pretend to be somebody they're not. Angela's children can see the talents they have and are empowered to express themselves.

Re-BOOT Activity: Sample Relationship Agreement

This is a sample relationship agreement that you and your significant other can use to reboot your relationship. Please feel free to edit this agreement to fit the specific terms you want in your unique relationship. If you wish to have a nontraditional or open relationship, express those terms so you are both on the same page. No two couples are the same; tailoring this agreement to suit *you* will require sitting down for an open review and rewrite to make it all yours.

This is a love agreement between _____ and _____.

For as long as we align in life and love, I promise to share openly in both my happiness and hardships.

I agree to be authentic and honest, even when it would be easier not to be.

I will be present for you and listen to you before answering, even if I must meditate on the answer for a day. I will always get back to you with a heartfelt, true response.

I promise to learn your love language and honor both your need to be held and your need to be free.

I will continue to share about my triggers, I will honor yours, and together we will agree upon code words when a trigger shows up. Then we can stay congruent and work through our past triggers together in love and freedom.

I will always keep my heart open to you and share my vulnerable truths.

I will be here until the time that you and I no longer align or move to a different plane. If for some reason our values and lifestyle desires no longer fit, I promise to keep our secret time and memories just ours. I can love you close or from afar and want to support who you truly are.

I promise to assume you have only the best intentions, and instead of jumping to conclusions, I will always ask and be open with you.

I will show up for all the date days, nights, and weekends you wish for. I understand that in our life there will be seasons where we may need to focus on other things; I promise to be there and enjoy you even if we stay home, roll up our sleeves, and get through a rough spot.

I found you and love your individual and unique true essence; therefore, I will always support you in your full life expression of hobbies, studies, and career passions.

I will always be open to discussion about our intimacy and happy to enjoy time experimenting and discovering with you.

I will check in with you when you are pushing me away. If you are hurting over other life issues, I will give you love and connection as well as breathing space when you need it.

I am wildly and beautifully imperfect and have the most perfect love for you. I thank you for loving me for all my parts, faults, flaws and all, just as I love you.

I will love you in form and in freedom. That being said, I will honor your individuality and self-expression as well as our time together. Both are necessary and incredible parts of our relationship.

I promise we will be humans in this and may have our fights or disagreements. Let's talk them through and agree to get further input from an agreed-upon therapist, interventionist, or relationship coach if the time is ever needed. Also, I agree to incredible make-up sex for occasional disputes.

I will do my very best to keep you safe, loved, and above all else honored.

I will never threaten to leave this sacred agreement. We may agree to disagree or together edit, review, add to, or delete portions of this agreement as the seasons of our life and love progress.

Above all else, I promise to love you, to learn with you, and to live passionately enjoying each magic moment with you.

Signed,

_____ and _____
Spouse/Partner   Spouse/Partner

I also like a book titled *Conscious Uncoupling* by Katherine Woodward Thomas for couples who are not able to make it, especially if they have children. It helps you see how you can own your part of the relationship not working out—without letting it upset the rest of your life.

For other resources for relationships, I have a resource section in this book, and the most current updates can be found on my website. My goal is to make sure that as you heal on your terms, you can connect to as many resources as possible.

🎁 *My Gift to You* 🎁

Is Self-Doubt stopping you from your BEST Relationship EVER?

Go from Self-Doubt to Self-Love so that you are able to give and receive love freely.

Anything worth having or keeping requires some work and strategy. It is important to not give up when your self-doubt shows up. One of the most important things you can bring to your current or new relationship is your BEST SELF. That means putting in the self-work.

How would you like to get THREE TIMES the results twice as fast?

For my readers I am making a special offer, take the BEST RELATIONSHIP QUIZ and receive the top 20 ways to improve or embark on the BEST RELATIONSHIP with yourself and your loved one.

Go to www.SheilaMac.com/bestrelationship.

CHAPTER 4

THE MANY MASKS OF ABUSE

Nicole is a client of mine in her early thirties who continues to grapple with the abuse that happened to her when she was younger.

Nicole was a great student, but in middle school, her friends started to pick on her because she wore layers and layers of clothes. Even in summer, when it was a hundred degrees, she would wear jeans and T-shirts and big, baggy sweatshirts. She didn't keep up with her hygiene and appearance—she didn't wash her hair often and never wore makeup—which was a big deal among the group of teenage girls who all wanted to fit in with their classmates.

Even though Nicole is a beautiful woman and was a lovely young girl, she worked very hard to keep herself concealed so her looks wouldn't be noticed.

It turns out that her father had been abusing her for years. Her father was an alcoholic, and when he was drinking, he abused Nicole physically, mentally, emotionally—and sexually. When he wasn't drinking, her father presented as a very kind and loving father and everybody thought he was a caring family man, devoted husband, and highly respected member of the community. Nicole kept his secret for years, as long as she could remember, fearing what could happen if she didn't—to her or to her two young sisters. She used to think, *At least they share a room, so he'll never get them alone.*

One night, Nicole's father got really drunk at home. He said terrible things in front of Nicole, her mom, and her sisters. In his ranting and raving, he threw things around the house, hit her mom, and then took off in a rage. As Nicole knelt by her mom, holding an ice pack to her bruised cheek, she breathed a silent sigh of relief that he'd left before it got even worse.

That night, after he drove off from the house, Nicole's father was pulled over and arrested for a DUI.

Nicole's aunt came over to help her mom try to post bail. As

Nicole watched them desperately try to help her abuser, she spoke up: "No, we can't do this! Leave him in there."

Because he was in jail and she finally felt safe—and because she felt he had shown his true colors in front of other people—Nicole did an incredibly brave thing and told her family of the abuse she had suffered at the hands of her father. It took her years to have the courage and strength to be able to shed light on the situation, but she was ready to put an end to it. Nicole didn't want to live with the terror, pain, and shame anymore.

"You're lying!" her mother accused.

"How dare you say that about your own father?" her aunt said.

The two women she had trusted with her deepest, darkest secret let her down when she needed them the most. They threw a couple of items of clothing at her, called her ugly names, and proceeded to kick her out of the house.

At age fourteen, Nicole was on her own.

She went to stay with a friend whose parents took her in. They helped her file a report against her father and took her to testify in court. The rest of her family, who had refused to help her and, in fact, hurled more abuse at her, continued to blame Nicole for her father's actions, and they stopped all communication with her. When the father got out of jail, Nicole's family moved away and never bothered with her again.

ABUSE HURTS

Nicole's story is one of injustice. It's ridiculously mind-boggling that this can—and does!—happen. Why would this young girl make up anything like that? And worse, why would her family—the people who are supposed to love and protect her in the first place—start this abuse and then, when it came to light, abuse her further by abandoning her?

Nicole now has built a beautiful life of her own (which you'll learn more about at the end of the chapter). Her friends have become trusted family members, and she is still happy that she freed herself and hopes that in sharing that truth her sisters were spared from the abuse she had to endure.

Sadly, the fact of the matter is that abuse happens all around us.

Abuse may be physical, which involves violence; verbal, where the abuser says things that cause their victim to shut down; sexual, where any sexual act is performed on another person without their consent; or even neglect, where a child or other dependent person's needs are not taken care of.

Adults may abuse children, whether those adults are parents, family members, teachers, coaches, or officials. Adults may abuse other adults, including elder abuse. Children may abuse other children—or even adults, too. There may be abuse at home, with a husband or significant other. An abusive parent may still be pulling strings, controlling their adult children. There can even be different levels of abuse at work.

When you're experiencing abuse—whether that's at work, at home, in your religion, or in another capacity—it ruins your experience of that area of your life and seeps into other areas as well. That place, that person, even the activities or group of people associated with it don't bring you the same joy anymore.

You may love your job, for example, and you may have been totally called to that particular field, but being around that person at work and that terrible energy can lead to physical and emotional symptoms of stress and anxiety. It may be so bad that you get panic attacks, your blood pressure goes up, or you get sick more often because the situation is stressful and wears you down. You may experience depression or anxiety, whereas before you were happy to go to work in that field. One person can cause an entire group not to feel safe. And finding out that a part of your life isn't safe takes away from all the good parts of it.

No matter what type of abuse we're talking about or what form it may take, it is not acceptable.

Abuse crosses a line. Someone who is being abused most likely doesn't wonder *if* they're being abused; they may wonder, *Why me? How did I get into this dysfunctional situation? Do I deserve this?* To answer that person's unspoken question: no. You do not deserve this. And if you currently feel like you are in an unsafe situation, listen to your gut. Get out, any way possible. (If you need to get out of an abusive situation, go to the resources section at the end of this book and visit www.sheilamac.com for the most current resources that can possibly help.)

People who are stuck in abusive situations are afraid. They wonder, *Should I say something, or will that just make everything worse?*

Abuse is a sensitive subject. I have had clients and friends who have shed light on abuse and their family supported them 100 percent. I've also seen a few cases like Nicole's, where the person reporting the abuse was not believed. The more people who are able to discuss this topic openly, the easier it becomes for people—male or female—to report abuse and sexual assault. It is sad yet true that although some people believe this only happens to girls and women, it happens to boys and men as well—and is talked about even less.

Nobody wants to talk about it, but abuse affects so many people. And not talking about it just keeps it buried and hidden. It's important, instead, to shine a light, to tell your stories, and to not let anyone hide behind the shame that victims of abuse may feel in talking openly about their experiences.

Every time someone is strong enough to bring that truth out into the open and shine a light on it, they free themselves, and they free other people as well. This is why it's so important to talk about abuse in this book—if we don't talk about these issues, they stay hidden. When we do talk about them, it is sad and difficult and painful, but we also realize that we're not alone.

Let me be really clear: I do not take this subject lightly. Abuse is something that stays with you for the rest of your life. You can't shake it off easily. Eventually, though, you may reach the point where you can grieve the fact that an abusive situation happened, but you don't let that past disturb your present or future moments. That is the point where freedom is created. We can't control these situations, yet we can be in charge of how we respond and live through them.

My hopes, in including this chapter, are to acknowledge your resilience and help give you strength to use your experience as fuel to become an advocate. When you're able to do that, your mindset—the way you view your experience and what to do about it now—shifts. You can't change what happened; nobody can. If we could, we would—but we can't.

So how are you going to change the things you *can* control? It doesn't mean that abuse is acceptable. It is never okay. But it is okay to release yourself, empower yourself, by telling your story.

MY STORY

I've experienced abuse myself, not only at home (which I'll tell you about a bit more in a later chapter) but also at school.

When I was eight years old and in the third grade, I had a teacher whose classroom was out of control. One little boy threw rocks at my friend Cindy, so I gave him a bloody nose. (Like I said, there was abuse at home; in my house, people solved their problems by fighting.)

The boy went crying to the teacher, and I got called into the principal's office for fighting. The principal didn't care that the kid had been throwing rocks that could hurt us or that we'd been telling the teacher about it for months. I got suspended.

When I came back to school, the same little boy started pulling at the straps of my training bra. Even as young as I was, I knew that was a violation and it wasn't okay.

I also knew that if I hit him again, I would get in even more trouble, so I went to the front of the classroom and told the teacher. The class was loud and rowdy, as usual. Spit wads flew across the room. I had to almost yell to make myself heard. Then the teacher told me, "Just take care of it yourself."

I was going to beat him up again, but that hadn't worked out so well last time, so I just ripped up the art project he'd been working on. I thought, "That'll make a point, but I'm not touching him so I can't get in trouble."

The boy—who was a tough bully until anyone stood up to him, at which point he went running to the teacher—told on me again.

The teacher grabbed my arm, her long, fake nails digging into my skin. She dragged me up to the front of the classroom, yelling at me. By the time she got me to the door, she was holding both of my arms and shaking me in front of the entire class. My vision blurred a little, but I could clearly see the blood dripping down my left arm where her nails had scratched me.

Eventually, I distracted her, and she finally let me go. I ran home, crying all the way. I didn't even look both ways when I crossed the street.

I stayed home for three days after that. When I came back, though, the principal and the school board came out and interviewed me and all the other students. That teacher got fired—and nobody ever picked on me at school again.

BREAK THE PATTERN, BREAK THE SILENCE

Sometimes it feels like if we can just figure out *why* someone is abusive, we can fix them or make them change.

Do they have a mental disorder that causes them to be abusive? Were they abused? What happened to this person to make them in any way compelled to do such a terrible thing to another human being? When does it stop?

There are patterns that show up with that type of abuser: they are controlling, overbearing, and they will often make sure there's no access to funds or to friends and family, so it feels like there's no way out. When a woman is being abused at home, her abuser may control the money or control her and make her feel too scared to think she could ever leave. That's not normal. Whether it's caused by codependency, a personality disorder, or other mental illness, it is not normal to abuse somebody you care about—or anybody else. Something is not right, and you don't have to diagnose it or give it a name other than that: abuse.

Physical abuse always carries a component of emotional or psychological abuse. The woman believes she could be killed if she tries to leave or she believes she deserves the abuse. Some women fear for their life just thinking about escaping. Many times, women in abusive situations may cover their fear because admitting it to someone else would lead to more abuse. In some cases, women hide their fear so well that even their own family is not aware of their situation. Sometimes they don't even admit anything even when the police get called in because they fear the abuse that will happen after the police leave.

A friend of mine from a very well-to-do family found herself living in fear for her life and that of her unborn child. Her husband physically abused her, and even when she was pregnant, the abuse continued. During her pregnancy, she kept showing up in the hospital with broken bone after broken bone. Her husband even stabbed her dog. After the baby was born, the husband locked the mother and child in the house when he left. She and the baby weren't allowed outdoors.

Eventually, after gathering up all her courage, my friend contacted an organization that packed up her and her baby, took her to another state, and set her up to start over. Even though her family was well off, she didn't ask them for money, because she feared for their safety if they got too involved.

If you are experiencing abuse, not much can be done until you are ready to break the silence and deal with the consequences. And if the abuse has gone on for a very long time, you may not be able to even imagine what's on the other side of doing that. It's easy to say, "It'll get better," but that may be difficult to comprehend when faced with such an enormous first step.

You may need to get help to break those patterns, but the first step has to come from you. You have to reach the point where you say, "I've had enough. I deserve better than this, and I'm ready to get out of this situation. I'm not going to pretend it didn't happen or hide it or cover for the abuse anymore."

When you get to that point, the minute you break the silence, people will help you get out. Friends, family, neighbors, even people you've never met are waiting and willing to help you leave that situation. But nobody can get you out of there until you're ready to walk out with them. That's the self-work, and it's really, really hard.

If you are thinking about breaking that silence but you're held back, you can begin by working on putting boundaries in place for your life.

BUILD YOUR BOUNDARY-SETTING MUSCLES

If you're being abused, your boundaries have been broken and you may feel like you don't have any limits in place, anywhere in your life. But with awareness that life can be different, you can see healthy relationships, healthy families, or healthy work environments and know that those are possible for you, too.

Love does not have to look like this. Your job or home life does not have to be like that. You are worthy and valuable, and you deserve a very different type of normal.

That awareness and a dose of self-love will allow you to begin to break that pattern. It will build you up to have the strength to break the silence. Once you start to shift what's okay, you also start to build boundaries, even if just a little bit at a time.

Walking away from a relationship that no longer serves you is huge. It's scary. There's a time between when you first walk away from unbalanced, unhealthy relationships when you're alone in this lonely place. But you realize, "I didn't like what they did, and it doesn't serve me. It's not aligned with who I'm becoming." Many women are afraid to be alone or go through this rejection from people who, unfortunately, may not believe you or may side with your accuser.

When you start to honor yourself, however, you will stop attracting those kinds of people in your life.

When you walk away from the people who don't treat you right, in any way, shape, or form, and surround yourself with your friends and family and people who love you and lift you up, you start to build a muscle—your boundary-setting muscle. Even small things are progress as you work on boundaries, strengthening that muscle so that you can set firm limits that will keep you from returning to the unhealthy situation—or moving into another, similar one.

You may want to practice what you're going to say so you set the boundary in a loving yet firm way. Prepare what you're going to say and repeat it, just like you use affirmations, so it comes out automatically. "No, that's not an acceptable thing to say to me. I'm ending this conversation now." Or, "No, I'm not going to be able to make it to that event. Thank you for the invitation."

Part of building that boundary-setting muscle is getting used to saying no—which then allows you to say yes to something more important.

Say yes to your yoga practice or time with your children versus saying yes to working overtime or volunteering for something you don't have the bandwidth for, that doesn't even interest you, or that you're "supposed" to do. Instead, say yes to what you really enjoy now. It could be meditation, singing, or studying personal development—anything that makes you happy. When you say yes to more of those things, you will align with and attract people who are also aligned with your values now.

On the other side of that tunnel of fear and loneliness is a new boundary—one on how you want to spend your time and who you value in your life. You value yourself first and then the other people you are aligned with. Your true north, your happiness, will bring you to the peer groups and relationships you need to support you as you continue moving forward.

If this seems easier said than done, it is. You may not be able to do it all on your own—and you don't have to. Friends and family may be able to help, but you may also want to consider professional help, both with overcoming the aftereffects of abuse and with setting boundaries. There are different therapy groups and relationship groups that can explore different ways to deal with abuse. And there's no way of knowing how long it will take. It could be a month; it could take six years. Therapists can't fix their patients, because you have to do the work and be willing to change, but they can help you set healthy limits.

HAVE A BACKUP PLAN

It's also important to have a backup plan in place so you know that you can survive if you walk away.

Unfortunately, this often comes down to having some money of your own set aside. I wish it wasn't about money, and in a perfect world it wouldn't be (in a perfect world, no one would ever face abuse!), but that can definitely be a factor in these situations. Money can be used as a form of control. If a woman is living paycheck to paycheck, or if she stays home to support the children, and she depends on having that second income, a man may use his contribution to feel like he has authority in the situation. An abusive boss or coworker may feel like he won't be confronted because he knows that she doesn't want to risk losing her job.

If you can create leverage—a backup business, a side gig, even selling things at the swap meet like I did—then you take back some of that power. If you can't change the situation—if you aren't ready to leave with your children or if reporting it is going to cost you your job anyway—then find something else that gives you enough to get the heck out. The situation is not serving you, and you deserve better than that.

This gives you the power to draw a line in the sand and say, "There are certain things that are not okay. If they continue, I'm going to leave." And know that you'll be fine.

I had a job with a boss who was very abusive to women. I never accepted any of his advances or let him get away with any misbehavior—and he didn't like that. I needed that job, but I wasn't willing to take that at work.

One day, I felt something wrong inside—it later turned out to be a kidney stone—and I told him, "I need to go to the emergency room."

He told me, "If you leave now, you're fired."

I did what was best for my health, and I walked out.

I had already started my gift store part time, and I was saving up money, so I knew I was good at what I did. Staying at that job wasn't the best situation for me and, in a way, the negativity forced me out—but that allowed me to start working for myself full time.

Sometimes it feels like we're trapped in abuse and hardship. Other times, it can feel like the reality is that you're being pushed out of a situation—a job, a community, even a marriage. But when there's abuse, you don't belong there. You have something bigger, something better waiting for you on the other side of that. You have a more important job, or an opportunity that's going to serve more people, or a relationship that is going to bless you and others in a bigger way.

I'm in no way condoning what that abusive person did to you, but they also played a role in helping you move on faster. When you look at the bigger picture, you will see that you are destined for something bigger than your small-minded abuser could ever imagine.

WHAT TO DO IF YOU SUSPECT THAT SOMEONE YOU KNOW IS BEING ABUSED

You may not have turned to this chapter because you are being abused but because you suspect that someone you know may be trapped in an abusive situation—but you don't know for sure.

Sometimes, both people fall into the pattern of abuse. It becomes a dance between two people. There's the person abusing and the person who becomes codependent on that abuser because they've set it up that way. Their needs are being fully met by this person, but they're so controlled to the point where they can't just open the door and walk out.

There may be different types of abuse happening, but the pattern is there—and the person being abused falls into those patterns, too.

I had a neighbor who was being abused. One night, it sounded really bad, so I called the police. The next day, her face was black and blue and she had a bloody lip, but she refused to press charges on her boyfriend. She was in denial, she was financially dependent on him, and she was too terrified for her safety to think about leaving.

Again, if you or someone you know is in an abusive situation where it's so bad you don't have a choice—you have to get out or you're going to die; they risk being killed—my website has resources for places that can help get you out quickly and safely. Go to www.SheilaMac.com/stopabuse or call the authorities right away.

A woman in such a controlling, abusive relationship may not

have access to this book. You can share it with her—but you can help her in other ways, too.

You can reach out. A quick compliment, like, "What a cute puppy," or, "Oh, you have such a beautiful flower bed," starts to form a connection. Bringing over a treat and introducing yourself creates an opening. You don't have to go inside the house or become best friends; you're just making sure she knows, "I'm here."

If you recognize or suspect that something is going on, you don't want to just say, "I called the cops and nothing happened, oh well, she'll just have to deal with it."

Now, I don't actually believe you'll think anything like that; it's actually hard *not* to want to help when you know what abuse feels like in some form or another. But people are afraid. Nobody wants to call the police or make waves; you don't want to make the situation worse. But that silence and fear of judgment or retaliation keeps that woman in a situation where she fears for her life.

When your intuition tells you something is dangerous, you can't ignore it.

Be aware. Keep your eyes open. Listen for details. You're not being nosy; you're listening for things said and unsaid, looking for bruises or off actions. Then you can have a friendly conversation. You can give them this book or a guide to other resources that are available.

You never know where that call for help will come from.

For my daughter's twentieth birthday, we went to a mall in

Santa Barbara, to go shopping and out to lunch. After lunch, we stopped by the restroom before trying on clothes.

From the next stall, I heard my daughter say, "Come look at this."

I was instantly on alert.

Someone had left a note in the stall saying they were being abused and couldn't get away. They asked for help and left their address. My daughter read that and said, "Mom, this doesn't feel right. We have to do something."

We stopped her birthday celebration to act on what we'd found. I was so proud of her for not thinking about herself at all; she only thought of how she could help this person who was reaching out in perhaps the only way possible.

We reported the note to mall security. We notified the police and asked for a welfare check at the address.

If you're not sure exactly what's going on, but you suspect that abuse may be taking place—as in this instance—you can call the nonemergency police phone number, request a welfare check, and the police or social services will send someone out to follow up. Let the officer know why you are requesting this check. Do you hear yells, things being thrown, calls for help, or what sounds like punches or slaps? The law agency can prioritize and expedite a call based on your honest explanation about why you are concerned.

We don't know the results because they don't report back, but they did say that they checked up on that address to see if someone was being held against her will. We'll never know for sure what happened, but doing *something* can save a person's life.

APPLYING THE BOOTS FORMULA TO ABUSE

Whether you are breaking your silence or helping someone else escape her pattern of abuse, the BOOTS Formula can help you walk through it.

BEING

Who are you Being in a situation where there's some form of abuse? We've talked about some of those different situations, and there are more than we could ever think of or write about. In any of those situations, there's a person who's being abusive and one who is being mistreated. Who you decide to be to get through this is so important. You need to find your strength to be able to get out; you need to be *strong* and show up for yourself first.

ORIENTATION

When you look at where you are—in an abusive situation—you also look at where you want to be. That may involve looking backward, at what your relationships, home, or work was like before you ended up in this situation and then looking at how it got to where it is now. This may be uncomfortable, confronting the truth, but you have to be really honest about what's happening.

Then you think of where you want to go—and how to get there.

You're going to take personal responsibility for controlling every aspect you can. If someone drinks every Sunday during football season, and they get abusive when they drink, then you can choose not to be home on Sundays. You can say, "If you drink, I'm going to leave." You can't control everything, and you can't control the other person, but you can control where you place yourself. Maybe that means being in a public place if you have to talk to your abuser, so that other people are around. Maybe that means having somebody on the other end of the phone or having them come over to support you. Maybe that means getting outside help because you recognize that the situation is bigger than you can handle on your own.

You can start changing who's in control of the situation by changing the pattern.

ORDER OF OPERATIONS

What are the steps you're going to take to get from where you are to where you want to be? The most important one is the first: recognizing that you are not going to allow the abuse to continue. Then look at what happens next: Do you need to have an exit strategy? Do you need to go to therapy? What other support or groups do you need? If this continues or gets worse, if you need to get out, what is the order? Do you need to save up or start talking to people? Do you need to go to therapy or set up a plan?

Your Order of Operations is going to be based on what outcome you want and what you're willing to accept into your life.

THINKING

Think about your best self, whether that was what it looked like before your current situation, or where you want to be in relationships or business or wherever this is happening. Picture that and work toward that end.

And acknowledge the good in the steps you're taking along

the way. Maybe you're the best teacher on the planet but the principal is abusive, or you don't like the way the school disciplines the children. Look at the good part—you know you're an amazing teacher, and you love working with these kids. Set the goal of either staying there and working through this situation, seeing if you can make changes, or of teaching at another school that is more aligned with you and has teaching methods you agree with.

You deserve to have your ideal life. You do not have to accept this treatment, from *anyone*. See yourself as the best you can be in the situation as it is now—and then how you want it to be.

STEPPING UP

Now you're stepping into that abusive situation—into that relationship or uncomfortable work situation—by stepping *out* of it. You're willing to do the work, but you're also putting your best foot forward. You're challenging yourself to get help, and you're really stepping into reviving that healthy part of yourself. That abusive person's actions have nothing to do with you. You're going to step out of that and into something even better. You're going to step into the choice to do things differently and find your own happiness.

FROM AN ABUSIVE ROCK BOTTOM TO MOMENT OF EMPOWERMENT

Let's catch up with Nicole, whose story we told to open this chapter:

Now in her thirties, Nicole's life has turned out very well. The love and support of her friend's family who took her in helped to ease the deep hurt of her family choosing the side of her abuser over their own daughter. Those feelings have never completely disappeared, and she still has conflicting feelings about family, but she has rebuilt herself to be successful—and to use her experience to help others in similar situations.

Nicole was able to free herself from that situation by speaking the truth. Today, she acknowledges that the consequences that came from that action are better than the consequences of staying in an abusive situation would have been. Her voice changed her life—and now it's changing others' lives as well.

Nicole works as a volunteer for a beautiful program called Courage House, helping children escape the sex trafficking trade. She helps these kids get a home to stay in and begin rebuilding their lives. They get access to counseling and psychological treatment. They get guidance. Because she has some understanding of what they've been through, Nicole's compassion helps her reach these kids and make a huge difference in their lives.

Through her volunteer work, Nicole has adopted an entirely different family into her world, and she's given meaning to the difficult situation she had no control over as a child.

Re-BOOT Activity: Know the Signs

If you feel you're in an abusive relationship, chances are you're right.

The signs of abuse are not always obvious. Abuse can be subtle, and it is more than physical; abuse often involves controlling someone's mind and emotions as much as hurting their body. Usually, in fact, physical abuse isn't what comes first. The abuse can creep up slowly. A putdown here or there. An odd excuse to keep you away from family or friends. The violence often ramps up once you've been cut off from other people. By then, you feel trapped.

Being abused can leave you scared and confused. It can be hard for you to see your partner's actions for what they really are. If you're afraid of your partner, that's a big red flag. You may be scared to say what you think, to bring up certain topics, or to say no to sex.

Signs of abuse in the workplace can involve forcing you to work long hours with low to no pay, yelling at you, or refusing to complete a referral for a new position. If your boss acts like they own your life and they neglect your needs as a human being, that is abuse.

Here are some additional signs that you are in an abusive situation:

Your partner bullies, threatens, or controls you:

- Accuses you of having an affair
- Blames you for abuse
- Criticizes you
- Tells you what to wear and how you should look
- Threatens to kill you or someone close to you
- Throws things or punches walls when angry
- Yells at you and makes you feel small
- Lies to you, often about things that don't even matter, to steal your free time and own your attention

Your partner controls your money:

- Keeps cash and credit cards from you
- Puts you on an allowance and makes you explain every dollar you spend
- Keeps you from working whatever job you want
- Steals money from you or your friends
- Won't let you have money for basic needs like food and clothes
- Buys him or herself nice things and never considers your needs, wants, or desires

Your partner tells you who you can or cannot visit or be friends with:

- Keeps close tabs on where you go and whom you go with
- Makes you ask for permission to see friends and family
- Embarrasses you in front of others, which makes you want to avoid people
- Follows you everywhere or tracks you on the cell phone or through surveillance cameras
- Questions your every move and decision
- Wants to know every detail of your day, yet shares nothing of theirs

Your partner starts hitting you and physically harming you or your loved ones/pets:

- Abandons you in a place you don't know
- Attacks you with weapons
- Keeps you from eating, sleeping, or getting medical care
- Locks you in or out of your house
- Punches, pushes, kicks, bites, pulls hair
- Hurts family pets, is mean and cruel to children, neighbors,

or others

Your partner requires sex on demand:

- Forces you to have sex
- Makes you dress in a sexual way
- Makes you feel like you owe them sex
- Has an STD they don't mention and still forces themselves upon you
- Refuses to honor your birth control or safe sex requests
- Announces he or she is getting tubes tied or having a vasectomy out of the blue (This may be a sign of multiple relationships or families, or partners with unprotected sex)

No matter what, fear is never present in a healthy relationship.

If you see these signs in even one area, it is one too many. In some cases, therapy or intervention could help, but if you are willing to change and the other person is not ready, it may be in your best interest to seek a community and guides to help you walk away.

I have discussed boundaries in a few chapters, but it bears repeating: if your boundaries are not being honored, it's time to seek additional help. As painful as it sounds, you need to get support on walking away from a difficult and abusive situation. If you feel like you're being abused, there's a good chance you may be, and it's worth getting help. In the resources at the back of this book, I have a list of referrals to programs and agencies designed to help you get out of abusive relationships.

🎁 *My Gift to You* 🎁

Dear Readers,

If you or a loved one is in the center of an abusive situation. I have a free guide called: ***Your Right to Be Safe—A Guide to Re-BOOTING After Dealing With An Abusive Situation***.

Go to www.SheilaMac.com/AbuseFree.

···················

CHAPTER 5

···················

MONEY MATTERS (FINANCE)

Geneva showed up at my vacation rental with a car full of her belongings, everything she hadn't been able to fit in her small storage unit down the road. She told me she'd been moving from one vacation rental home to another, occasionally staying at friends' homes in between.

She'd felt guided to visit me and had booked my rental for three days but noticed it was available for the month. "I don't have all the money at once," she told me. "Can I pay as I go?" I couldn't help but tell her yes; I knew she was in the right place.

After she unpacked and got settled in, we sat outside on the deck for coffee and snacks. Soon, Geneva started to share about her own rock-bottom situation. She told me she used to own a beautiful three-bedroom home and had been happily married with two grown sons. She had worked part time for the school district and her husband was a props designer.

She started to cry a little but tried to hide it as, with a deep sigh, she continued.

Geneva said she really loved that man and thought she had a rock-solid, honest husband. He was a bit of a slob and sometimes got angry with the kids, but he was a good provider and always very loving. She always trusted him and kept herself busy working and raising their kids.

One day, the power went out at the house. When Geneva called the company to have a repairman come out, they told her that her service had been turned off due to unpaid bills. When her husband—who'd always paid the bills—got home, he explained that it had been a misunderstanding and he'd taken care of it, putting the bills on auto pay so she didn't have to bother with them.

Soon after that, Geneva went to make a phone call and discovered that the family's cell phone service had been disconnected. She was upset and concerned, so she drove over to her husband's job site. They told her that he hadn't been assigned to that site that day—even though that's where he told her he'd been working for the past three weeks.

When he returned home, Geneva asked her husband, "How was work?"

"Great," he answered. "We got a lot done, and the project should be finished in a week or two."

She asked where he was working, and he told her the same site she had visited earlier that day.

That's when it all came out: for most of their marriage, instead of working extra-long hours, he was actually visiting his other family.

Yes, he had a girlfriend and, together over the last ten years or so of their marriage, he and she had three other children! Geneva had been minding her business, living what she felt was a pretty good and honest life, when BOOM! The bottom fell out from under her.

Then, just like that, her husband left her alone in the shambles of their old life. Because he'd been in charge of their money and paying the bills, Geneva hadn't realized how behind they were. Everywhere she looked, all she saw were final notices and bill collectors. They were upside down on the house, she didn't have enough money to get current on the mortgage, and her credit was ruined. She said she went into a deep depression from the emotional and financial fallout. She just didn't know what to do—she didn't even know where to start.

Geneva admitted that she drank too much for a while, oversleeping and calling out from her part-time work. When there was a downsizing wave, she was the first one to get fired.

At this point in her story, Geneva was in full tears, with little bits of laughter and waves of anger, too. As she mentioned her ex, she slammed her fist on my park bench.

When she came to stay with me, Geneva was working for a temp agency and taking part-time cleaning jobs on the side. She joked about how she'd seen a van advertising a topless maid service and admitted she was inches away from calling to apply, just for the extra money.

It was just a joke, yet it spoke to a serious feeling: how on earth could she ever get ahead?

THE TRUE COST

Situations we can't control or predict, ones that have serious financial consequences, happen more often than we'd like.

We don't want to believe that this can happen to us. It's not something you'd ever want to think about or prepare for—Geneva had certainly never thought it was possible—but if the unexpected happens, you may find yourself in a financial pinch or even a financial catastrophe.

Your financial circumstances change throughout your life, but when those changes are accompanied or even caused by a major life shift, that can lead to a rock bottom.

Bouncing back from a financial rock bottom consists of three steps, which we'll look at in this chapter:

STEP ONE: Evaluate where you are financially. (The activity at the end of the chapter walks you through this step.)

STEP TWO: Use your resourcefulness to get where you need to be to support yourself and your family, if you have children.

STEP THREE: Once you have that stability, you can start looking for other opportunities to invest and potentially grow your money.

FACE THE DRAGON

Whether you are going through a catastrophic event or financial hardship, the first step is to take an honest look at your financial picture.

Maybe your husband did the finances. Maybe you did the

finances and he helped do something else—but now you have to take over everything. If you've never had to manage your finances entirely on your own—or even if you have been in charge of your finances—you can learn how to manage them better.

When you're going through the finances, it can feel like you have nothing left over after paying your bills. You almost want to give up or not even look, just throw the bills in a drawer and worry about them when money shows up. Then, once the drawer is full, you throw them on the floor of the closet, wondering where the money is going to come from. Your financial situation gets worse and worse until you can't even qualify to buy a vacuum.

It happens. Financial stress is hard and scary.

But there's something really empowering about taking an honest look at your financial situation and learning where to go from here. I call this facing the dragon.

If you are behind in your bills, there are ways you can negotiate or make arrangements for your payments. People are so afraid to just pick up the phone and call the bill collector or credit card company. Call American Express and say, "Hey, I had a death in my family, and I need more time to pay." Oftentimes they'll give it to you.

If your credit isn't good, I strongly suggest working with a credit repair service. Most of these services will actually write letters to your creditors on your behalf, removing or consolidating payments. After they get down to any bills that cannot be removed, many of them will actually get on a three-way call and help you through the negotiations to lower your payments.

If you are going about this alone, it may be best to have a friend or family member that you trust get on the line with you or review what to say prior to calling in.

I have worked with hundreds of clients who've had to repair their credit to qualify for a home loan or who had to rebuild their score due to a rock-bottom scenario. They all said it was far easier than they had imagined and that, once they got through the first call or two, they no longer had the stress or fear.

Our minds tend to jump to the worst-case scenario very quickly, but once we face the dragon, take that really painful first step, and do the work, it's a huge relief as some of that stress disappears. Taking this first step will give you a sense of getting back into control as you rebuild your financial house.

But it doesn't happen all at once. If this is where you've hit rock bottom, it takes time to get through it and start going back up. What you have to do isn't really hard, but it might take a few days, weeks, or even months of making calls and arranging payment plans until you're back in the driver's seat.

ASK FOR HELP

Just because you are learning to manage your finances yourself doesn't mean that you won't need help. You don't have to do it all on your own.

One way to make a financial situation feel less scary is to get advice on how to handle it. A financial planner, credit counselor, money manager, accountant, or attorney may be able to help you come up with a strategic plan. If you can't afford to see one of these professionals, or if you want to take more control, the activity at the end of this chapter will help you come up with your own plan (and you can visit the resources section of my website at www.SheilaMac.com/finances for links to free, basic financial services).

You are disempowered when you don't have a plan. The longer you go without a plan, throwing bills in a drawer, the more you mess up your credit and cause other trouble in your life that you don't need. The sooner you face it and do the work, the better. When you do have that plan in place, you just follow it. It's cleaner that way, and it's empowering.

THE IRS OR...THE PRESIDENT?

When I was twenty-four years old and my daughter was a few months old, I was in the second year of running my gift store business. I had figured out how to design the store, make it beautiful, and serve the customers, but I really sucked at accounting.

I was making enough money, so accuracy wasn't a big deal for me; I didn't worry about counting every penny. I knew what my account balance was, but when I did my state taxes, I would just round off the numbers for income and expenses. I didn't know you aren't supposed to do that!

One day, four people wearing black suits and almost-invisible headsets walked in. They were not my typical gift store customers. My stomach dropped; had I screwed up on my taxes? Was the IRS coming to take away my store—or me? I considered grabbing the baby and running, but instead remembered to follow the training I gave my staff and treat every customer like a movie star.

I'm glad I didn't run—(then) President Clinton walked into my store! He had been speaking at Glendale Community College nearby and then visited some local businesses. The suits were his Secret Service staff.

I gave him a gift of Crabtree and Evelyn fragrances for men and the top-selling ladies fragrance for Hilary. He held the baby and we took a picture (that was sadly lost in the fire I told you about in a previous chapter).

The few minutes of fear I had when the suits walked in convinced me I needed someone else to manage my accounting. The next day, I hired a CPA. One of the first things he told me was, "You have to use real numbers. It's kind of a giveaway when everything ends in zero."

Ideally you can get the help you need when things are good, so you already have a plan in place in case things go bad.

BE RESOURCEFUL

A financial rock bottom can happen at any time and be caused by any number of situations.

Whether your life shift is planned or unplanned—an unexpected medical emergency, going through a divorce, death of a spouse or partner, or getting laid off from a job—that life shift is also causing a shift in your finances. To better deal with life circumstances, you may choose to shift from full-time to part-time work, resulting in lower income. The shift from two incomes to one or to simply having less income than you're used to requires both a psychological and financial adjustment.

If you lose a job, you can evaluate your situation and look for what you want to do next. But when you're not necessarily looking for a new job, or when a spouse loses his job and is going through an extended period of unemployment, or one of you goes back to school, you have to be resourceful in how you approach your life plan.

Tony Robbins says, "It's not the lack of resources, it's your lack of resourcefulness that stops you."

The resourceful person is going to fare so much better than the one who's not. Being resourceful is going to take you outside your comfort zone, but it also leads to thinking outside the box.

When I bought my little house, one of my friends told me, "You should just rent an apartment. You can't afford to fix up this house, and there's no way you're going to make an income from it."

She couldn't fathom how many times I had made successful real estate investments before with many other properties. A regular, nine-to-five office job would never pay me what I made investing in real estate. They said, "We love you. Good luck with that. We'll be here to help when you're ready to move into an apartment or need a job referral."

A month later, I had three different units that I had created out of this small place. I lived in one of them and rented out the others, making an average of $5,000 a month in a little cabin.

How did I do it? I sat down and created a mind map and then a vision dream board to really get clear on the possibilities. I knew from past experience that this was an area I could turn to when needed. I also did a rough estimate on the cost of the project and decided that if I did most of the labor myself, I would be able to make this project pencil, even on my shoestring budget! I knew design from my big store, so I did all the design work and painted the place myself.

Resourcefulness is so important. You can't wallow in the rock bottom and mourn the lifestyle that you no longer have. Instead, look for ways to replace your lost income and ask yourself:

- What can you do that other people haven't thought of? Do you have a unique idea, skill, or area of expertise?
- What can you make or find cheaply and sell, whether it's on Craigslist, eBay, Etsy, or Amazon?
- What previous experience do you have that will serve you in new endeavors?
- Who can you help? For example, if you've taught in the past or have a strong skill, perhaps you're interested in tutoring online. There are services that connect you with clients, so you don't have to spend money on an office or marketing; you just need an internet connection.

The most important question is, "How can *you* move from your rock bottom to someplace better?"

I've lived outside the box for so long that I don't even know there is a box. Join me in this better place!

INVESTMENT STRATEGIES

When you first start rebuilding a foundation to a new life or reinventing yourself after a financial rock bottom, you are the captain of your ship. Nobody else is going to steer it for you, just as nobody else will be as invested in your outcomes as you are. Many women think they can hand off control of their money and investments to someone without staying involved, but financial success is not going to just magically happen.

Only you have your best interest at heart. It's important to know that—even if it's very scary to contemplate how to manage your money, particularly if you've never done it before. And, even if you hire a financial advisor or money manager, you still need to stay involved in how they manage your money and ultimately you decide whether to follow the investment advice they provide.

A friend of mine, a life coach, called me about an emergency situation with a client of hers whom I'll call Betsy. Because of my experience in real estate, she asked if I would talk with Betsy about an investment she was planning to make.

Betsy was going to take out a loan for $200,000 to invest in building homes in another state. The lender was going to charge her 13 percent, but somehow—if the homes ever get built or actually exist—she could expect to make about $200 a month in income.

We spoke for a couple of hours, starting with easy questions like, "Have you done your due diligence?"

Betsy knew nothing about the company or the homes and had never been to the site.

As we talked, it came out that she'd recently gotten divorced and was having to adjust her lifestyle. This investment opportunity sounded like an easy way to make some money every month without having to do any extra work, but the company was preying on Betsy's desperation.

By the time we did the numbers on the loan, with no guaranteed return on investment, she was at a loss. But we looked at Betsy's budget and easily found places she could make small changes and save more than $200 a month. The only investment she needed was investing in changing her mindset.

Unfortunately, a lot of women feel that they have to jump at the first opportunity to earn money—but even though they think they're doing the right thing, it can lead to a bad place.

When considering investment strategies, you want to:

- Have caution—and make sure you have emergency savings first.
- Consider your options—lowering your expenses can often result in as much or more income than an investment.
- Talk to more than one person about different methods of investing.
- Have family, friends, or a CPA—someone you trust and who has a good track record with finances—review your plan before you pull the trigger…so you don't shoot yourself in the foot.
- Remember that if it sounds too good to be true: it is! There's working smarter and then there's someone conning you out of your hard-earned money.
- Check the Better Business Bureau to see if the company has good reports and to make sure there aren't any claims filed against the company.
- Call the resources or ask to speak to client references to see if they are still happy clients a year or so later.

- Before you sign a contract, review it with an attorney or someone experienced in the field. Read each line and if you don't understand something, get clarification. Also sign in a place with witnesses and all parties present or use DocuSign. I had someone alter a contract after my signature was in place and it cost me a fortune to prove. Lessons learned that way are hard and costly ones.
- Keep business to business, *especially* if doing business or any form of partnership with family or friends. Get legal contracts, put it all in writing, make sure that you are all on the same page, and get legal counsel *before* any problem happens so that nothing goes wrong. Losing family and friends is not worth the cost.

Doing your due diligence requires a little more work up front, but it ensures that you don't find yourself in a situation more desperate than the one you're trying to leave.

DO WHAT YOU KNOW

The best advice I can offer around investment is "Do what you know."

If you don't know anything about Bitcoin or cryptocurrency, that's probably not the best investment to start with. Stick with something you have studied or that you have past experience with. Ask yourself, "Where have I made money in the past?" What has produced money for you or somebody in your family who could help and mentor you? What resources and knowledge do you have?

For example, I know real estate. I've bought and sold twenty-seven buildings and properties and done 1031 exchanges. I do very well in real estate investment—making 40 percent or more on the cash flow side and quite a bit on my sales. On the personal side, I have the experience of remodeling and working with a construction crew at a job site. I know how to do that really well, so I'm not going to start investing in stock options.

I have a friend who does well with that type of investment, and she's offered to walk me through it. If I decide to take a chance on that new strategy, I'm going to start by investing a tiny amount—so little that if I lose it all because I make a mistake, I'll still be okay. Investing can be a gamble, but I'm reducing my risk by getting help from my friend who's great at making money this way.

LEARN FROM THE BEST

Along those lines, it's important to learn from the best people possible for your chosen strategy.

One way I've done that is by going to Platinum Wealth mastery, an event where top leaders in finance come out and teach you about finance and what's happening in the world. It's a small room with maybe a hundred people, and we learned directly from them. Steve Forbes and former President Clinton spoke, along with Harry Dent and Ray Dalio. It was a beautiful opportunity to learn about their perspective on that year's finances and how to invest.

We also went through our individual finances, looking at how we invested in our businesses and lives. A group of us from that event still meet for mastermind programs on a regular basis to keep ourselves on track with our finances. We stay in the community because we get so much out of it.

Learning from the best has helped me, as well as my clients and friends, to make some really good financial decisions.

APPLYING THE BOOTS FORMULA TO FINANCES

When getting yourself out of a financial rock bottom, you have to be clear on what you need and how you're going to get that.

BEING

Start, as always, by asking yourself who are you Being? And who do you need to show up as in order to get your life back into order?

Being a victim, somebody who got run over by life, is not going to get you out of this rock bottom. You have to be your strong self and show up for yourself, so you can get out of that place.

Are you in charge of your life, or are you going to let other people tell you what to do with your finances or investments?

You have to take charge. If you haven't played that role in this area of your life before, you can pull from other areas of your life where you're really good at being in charge. Take that personality trait and apply it to money and investment. We all have that leader inside of us. We are all capable of making a really sound decision.

Those decisions don't always happen in the middle of chaos, but if you can set aside the emotion for a moment to focus on what you really need, you'll know what's best for your situation. I like to do this by pretending. I have my coaching clients pretend to give a close friend advice to help her get through a difficult financial journey. You will be pleasantly surprised at the insight that shows up when you take the emotion out of the equation!

That way, when people start offering you the sun, moon, and stars to get their hands on your money, you won't give up everything you have. The person who isn't going through the emotional trauma would never say yes to that, so draw on that strength and take charge.

ORIENTATION

Face the dragon. Be realistic about how difficult and over-whelming financial rock bottoms can feel. Don't ignore them. And then own up to your part in getting to this place and take control over where you go from here.

The moment the blame game stops—even if it truly was a situation completely out of your control—that's the instant you become emancipated from the past. If someone else is in control of your present situation, you're not! So once you decide to truly take your power back, there is freedom in that simple choice.

Where are you and where do you want to go? It's not better or worse than it is; this is where you're at. Knowing where you are today gives you a starting point, and then you can make a map of the steps to take in order to get where you want to go.

You can also ask yourself, "What is it going to look like if I do this?" What will it really look like in six months, a year, two years? How will it affect your life then? What if something happens? You don't want to put everything in one basket, rely on that, and then have it not work out.

ORDER OF OPERATIONS

At this point, you're looking at the things that you need to get done and asking, "What is my next action?" You're going to look at the results and see where you need to change direction a little bit, but you have a target, you know where you're going, and you have an action plan.

This may be a big shift and you may have to work extra or put in some overtime, and that's going to be difficult. It does pay off—but it doesn't pay off in a day. You may have to be dedicated and put in the time and the work for a while. There's always the lag time between when you start to do something and when the results start to show up. You think, "I'm putting in so many hours and receiving nothing in return. I could just go sit at the beach and get the same results!"

But once you get past that point and reach equilibrium, things catch up and now you have a new identity in the financial area. On those days when you'd rather go to the beach, you have to stay and do the work. Then you'll start to see it explode and take off and all the results will finally start showing up—and it gets easier. *Then* you can take that time and celebrate and go to the beach.

THINKING

When you're in survival mode, you can't think straight. You don't even have time to think. You just need to know how you're going to survive. Your adrenaline is up, everything is heightened. You're scared, and it's a terrible place to make decisions from. But once you start to make small shifts, you can get yourself some footing on solid ground. This creates some breathing room so you can take the next small step—and take some time to think clearly about your future.

You have to have a vision and you need to walk into that, acting as if the outcome is guaranteed. You've got to own it, act as if, and believe it. You're putting your passion into it, and the vision is so clear you can see it, you can taste it, you can feel it and smell it. It's that real for you.

STEPPING UP

Having the vision is only the first step; you have to do the work that's required to get there. Focus on what you're going toward instead of what you're going through. You can use your energy to cry and worry and be upset, or you can use it to fuel your future and reinvent yourself and the new life that you desire.

FROM FINANCIAL ROCK BOTTOM TO MOMENT OF EMPOWERMENT

Remember Geneva from the story at the beginning of this chapter?

During the three months she ended up staying with me, I guided Geneva through the BOOTS Formula. After just our first discussion, the look in her eyes changed from that of a person who had given up to someone who had some hope. Each step in the process brought her to a more confident, happy place.

The first thing that Geneva had to do was decide who she was going to be now.

Initially, all she wanted to do was get back to the day before she found out, so she didn't have to deal with all of this fallout. But it happened, and there are no time machines to take you back.

Geneva was not responsible for her ex-husband's actions, and blaming him wasn't helping the situation. She also had to stop blaming herself for thinking she had a different family arrangement than what was actually going on. She had to forgive herself for missing things because she trusted her husband.

This awful thing happened to her, and she had to own her part and take personal responsibility for what she could change in her own life. She had to face the aftermath of the situation and acknowledge, "This is where I am now. These are my finances. This is what my situation really looks like."

Geneva was living day by day, not even paycheck to paycheck. She had to be really honest about where she was with all the different parts of her life—where she was before this event happened and where she wanted to be now.

She was paying a lot in rent for the storage unit to hang onto her things, but she didn't always know if she had a place to sleep at night. We first found a storage unit that was much cheaper, the first of many little steps like that so she could buy herself the breathing space and get through that desperate survival mode.

Geneva's credit wasn't good after all those missed bills, and she didn't have money for a deposit on an apartment, so she couldn't move forward until she got some cash flow and solid employment. Over our talks, we got into remembering her essence, talents, truths, taking her skills and strengths from her past, before she was a wife and mother, and pulling those forward. We looked at what she loves to do so she could do something she enjoyed—but she also needed to do something quick, to bring in some money and get back on solid ground.

Geneva is an incredible artist, and she was also very good at keeping her home in order. She loved being a mom, and she missed bringing her kids to all the after-school sports activities, socializing with the other moms, and volunteering in her community. I introduced her to an agency that hires home assistants and nannies, and she found a family that was in desperate need of help.

She ended up helping to raise three more young boys and loved every minute of that (and it didn't hurt that the job paid six figures the first year!). Geneva is still very close to that family, which is very involved with the art community. During her time with them, she got to do lots of projects with the kids and also took up photography on the side. Now, she's started her own professional photography business.

Geneva was able to reboot her Thinking and take back her power. She stepped into a new habit of thinking forward, of reinventing and redesigning her life, not looking back anymore. She had already reviewed that chapter of her life, gone through the emotions and expressed herself, so she put that part to sleep, allowing her to wake up and live her life.

Now, she's living the life she wants, thinking about the beautiful parts of every day and sharing it with her loved ones.

FIND THE GRATITUDE IN THE SITUATION

Even if you've had a financial crisis, how you show up is crucial. You have to face the things you need to do—but you don't have to give it all your time. Don't stay up all night worrying until you're sick and can't function. Don't feel that negativity. Go toward what you want to make happen; don't give all your energy to what you're trying to move away from.

It happened, and you have to admit it. But once you've made a plan for moving forward, that's all the attention it gets.

Once you've activated the BOOTS Formula, don't dwell on the rock bottom any more. Put your focus on gratitude and the good things that are happening because you've taken control of the situation. Don't wait to be grateful and happy after things sort themselves out. Don't put off your happiness. Enjoy the happy moments as they happen.

It's an empowering personal choice to make the best of the situation and to find the gratitude in it.

Re-BOOT Activity: Financial Check-In

This checklist will help you check that your finances and paperwork are in place (and show where you may need to take additional steps). This is especially important to review during or after a major life shift.

☐ I have reviewed my financial situation and, if necessary, discussed this with those closest to me.

☐ I have completed a budget and track actual monthly costs to my budget.

☐ I have _____ weeks/months of expenses saved in case of emergency.

☐ I have a plan to meet my goal of_____ by this date _____.

☐ I have a long-term savings plan and/or retirement plan.

☐ A list of my banking and financial accounts is located here: _____.

- ☐ I have completed my will and power of attorney (POA) and listed a durable power of attorney for financial, digital, and medical or other roles to people I trust, and I have a backup person listed for each role.
- ☐ The will is signed, notarized, and a copy has been given to those listed.
- ☐ My copy of my will is located here: _____.
- ☐ I have completed my living will (also called an advance care directive).
- ☐ I have named a healthcare advocate and a backup person.
- ☐ I have given additional information and notice to my doctor.
- ☐ I have discussed my wishes—what I want and don't want—with friends and family.
- ☐ I have discussed or written down the type of funeral or memorial service I desire and any instructions about burial or cremation.
- ☐ I have considered where and how I would like to be cared for if I were terminally ill and discussed this with those closest to me.
- ☐ The living will or trust is signed, notarized, and a copy has been given to those named or listed.
- ☐ My copy of my living trust/will is located here: _____.
- ☐ I have given this information to family members, friends, or legal advisors.

Insurance

- ☐ I have researched life insurance options and purchased the best possible plan for myself and/or my family.
- ☐ I have researched short-term disability and completed all steps.
- ☐ I have researched long-term disability and completed all steps.
- ☐ My copy of my policy is located here: _____.
- ☐ I have listed my personal details in case of emergency when

someone else needs to retrieve it (passwords, contact information, accounts, etc.)

Bonus Re-BOOT: Rebuilding Your Credit

When going through a life shift, a Credit and Finance Re-BOOT is
very common. Do your best to reduce expenses and limit credit
spending as much as possible.

First, understand your credit or FICO score. Most mortgage
companies use the FICO to determine your loan and interest rate.

Score Range Category

- 781—850 Super Prime
- 661—780 Prime
- 601—660 Non-prime
- 501—600 Subprime
- 300—500 Deep Subprime

Next, review the five biggest factors that impact your score:

1. Payment history—35 percent

2. Amounts owed—30 percent

3. Length of history—15 percent

4. New Credit—10 percent

5. Types of Credit—10 percent

Finally, do a credit and financial reboot:

- I have an action plan or am working with a reliable credit repair agency. This process usually takes ninety to 120 days depending on your score, ability to pay down debt or restructure, and your willingness to follow recommended action steps in a timely fashion.
- Do few to no credit inquiries if at all possible. Every time someone looks at your credit score, it gets an additional hit. If possible, offer to pay a deposit for new utilities in lieu of the inquiry.
- Check with your local credit union or bank to see if they can help you refinance your auto loan and save on your interest payments.
- Talk to your lenders sooner rather than later. Many student loans and installment loan companies offer deferment programs or a forbearance on your loan. Call and ask if you qualify for any hardship services they may offer.
- If your credit cards have high interest rates, and your score is in good standing, consider applying for a 0 percent interest, balance transfer card. There are credit cards now at 0 percent interest for up to fourteen months.
- Start (or stop) credit card autopay. Bill pay is a great way to be sure that you're not late on your monthly payments because it makes it easier to track all payments made. However, if you have been using autopay and your budget just took a huge hit, you may want to hit pause while you make payment arrangements or until you know that the funds are available, so you can avoid high fees.
- Check your subscriptions, especially those that are automatically charged on your credit card. Do you still need these items, or can you put them on hold for the short term?
- If you can't stop a charge, block that card. Call your bank or

financial institution and put a hold or block on the card until you can get the cancellation to go through.

Some of these steps may seem like a hassle, but the effort is worth it when you need to take your power back in this area.

I have also created a No-Cost, Ninety-Day Financial Reboot Action Plan.

🎁 My Gift to You 🎁

Dear Readers,

I have a GIFT that keeps giving for you! Go to www.SheilaMac. com/moneyreboot to receive a FREE video series on how to get out of debt and rebuild your credit. If you've been struggling with having more month at the end of your money and can't qualify for a vacuum cleaner on credit, this program is a special gift for you.

....

CHAPTER 6

....

WORKING HARD FOR THE MONEY (CAREERS)

I've gone to the same woman's spa since I was eighteen years old.

I first saw this oasis called Sheila's Spa in a magazine my dear friend Julie gave me when I was in a holding placement camp awaiting my emancipation hearing (that story to come, too!). Before I'd ever heard about vision boards, I cut out that article and put it on the wall over my bed. I told myself, "One day I know I'll go to Sheila's Spa—it even has my name on it!"

By the time I was eighteen years old, I was working at JPL and starting to sell things at the swap meet on the side. Finally, I was able to afford to go on my first trip to "Sheila's Spa" (although the owner, Sheila Cluff, renamed the spas The Oaks at Ojai).

Every single year since—often two or three times a year—I would stay at the spa, sometimes for a month or more. When I first started going, I could only manage to pay for a three-day weekend pass. I worked from the spa, running my businesses and enjoying the retreat. Sometimes I'd help with a couple of classes or with a program, as my way to give back. I came to know all these beautiful ladies from around the world. It was a woman's community, a safe place to just relax and connect.

This was truly my second family, and I have so much gratitude for the Cluff family and all the people who helped create the spa environment I called my second home.

The spa was open for more than forty-five years until it was caught in the Ventura fire and sustained so much damage that they had to permanently close. Until that day, it had been open 24/7—they literally hadn't closed their doors until the fire shut them down.

Some of the employees had worked at the spa since it first opened its doors, the only job they'd had for the bulk of their adult lives. It was a beautiful place to work and became like a second home for those employees.

And, just like that, it disappeared.

Everybody in the whole community lost their jobs—not just the spa, but other local businesses that depended on the people the spa attracted from all over the world to stay in their little town. Some of the employees had to relocate. And obviously, this wasn't planned. They all lost their income very suddenly, unexpectedly, and dramatically. They couldn't see it coming or make other plans.

After December 2017, all the women working at the spa had to reinvent themselves, start over, and rebuild their lives.

FROM SHIFT TO GAP

Not all career shifts are as dramatic as the one those women were thrust into—but most women will experience at least one career shift at some point in her life, if only as she moves into or out of the workforce.

Different career shifts may occur at different stages of life: becoming a mom and having to pull back or take time off from the workforce, moving back into a workplace after a considerable amount of time off where you may be dealing with a lot of changes, or confronting retirement. You may be moving from full time to part time or the other way around—or even going from paid work to volunteer work.

Whatever shift you are making, you are unlikely to find an even playing field.

Statistically, women get paid less than men. In 2017, the US Census Bureau determined that women working full time, year-round, earned only 80 percent of what their male counterparts earned.[1] That's a pretty big gap.

It's better than it was, but we still don't command the same salaries that our husbands, boyfriends, fathers, and brothers do. We're stuck with that. We're changing it, but in the meantime it's a reality, unfair as it may be.

Because the deck is still stacked against us, we women often have to work even *harder* to support ourselves and our families. In this chapter, we'll look at ways you can close that gap as much as possible, including learning how to find your soul-

---

1   https://www.census.gov/library/publications/2018/demo/p60-263.html

calling, supporting your career with education, volunteering, and being prepared for the multiple career shifts most women go through.

WHAT IS YOUR SOUL-CALLING?

When you have a change in career, whether it's a conscious choice to work less, a forced choice because your employer is downsizing, or you're making the shift toward retirement, the change is an opportunity to redirect your life and say, "Now it's going to be on my terms."

That is the time to follow your passion or what I call your soul-calling. Figure out the other things you can do. Evaluate your talents to see what you're good at and where you can make money. You might have a passion you want to pursue, even if you made your money in another industry. If you're open to the opportunity, your soul-calling can redirect you to something that is so much better than the job you didn't like that you only did for the money. (I'll show you how to determine what your soul-calling may be in the activity at the end of this chapter.)

Everybody has a talent. When you follow your talent and mission to help people, you will experience a kind of a pull or draw toward activities that utilize your talent. It's almost like you can't *not* do it. You keep finding yourself using that talent; it just comes out. You can't keep it locked up in a box.

We all wear different hats and work in different careers, but the strong talent that is your driving force is your own. When you're doing it, you could do it for free. Sometimes you *are* doing it for free, because that's how it shows up. You're not going to be able to get away from it. You can pretend. You can try to go do something else to make money. Maybe that pays more for the moment, to pay your bills, but in the long run you'll be continually drawn to your purpose.

That feeling of being drawn toward something means the activity aligns with your core values and your life purpose, the vision of who you are. It's the shoe that fits your foot. When you enjoy what you're doing, you think, "They're going to pay me for this? That's awesome!"

I have a client named Lady whose husband surprised her by asking for a divorce. He came home, said, "I'm in love with someone else," and he was done. One day everything was fine, and the next day, he was gone—leaving her alone with her three kids. She was caught totally off guard.

When she came to me to figure out what to do next, we looked at her skills, past experiences, and different options.

Lady told me how, when she was a young girl and teenager, she took cake-decorating classes—and her cakes won prizes and awards. She made beautifully decorated cakes that looked like famous people or Disney characters. She would sell them to her family and friends who wanted fancy birthday cakes. Sometimes Lady would bake these cakes for free and give them as gifts for the holidays, because baking is her passion.

Now that's what she does for a living.

She followed what seemed like the natural next step and started a cake-decorating business. Lady works out of a professional kitchen, baking sugar-free, gluten-free cakes for the health-conscious and regular ones for people without dietary restrictions—and the sugar-free ones cost even more than the regular ones! She's super happy, but she had to be resourceful and go back to her own skills. She probably wouldn't do so well designing a house, for example; but she can decorate a cake.

After the divorce, Lady didn't have the option of not working. She had kids to take care of and bills to pay. Now she's blessed with being able to finally live her passion. She was able to take back some of her power, to make a choice about what she does instead of letting that situation dictate how her life was going to go. She's in charge of what her career looks like.

BACK TO SCHOOL

Sometimes you may need to supplement your experience with additional education before you can pursue your dream career.

While I was working on the revisions of this book, I took some time off to go out to dinner. The restaurant was pretty empty, so I struck up a conversation with the hostess and waitress, who turned out to be two amazing ladies. Both Stacy and Judie are single moms, raising their children on the wages they earn at the restaurant.

Stacy confided that she had her first child when she was a child herself, at the young age of sixteen. She never graduated high school. Now, at forty-eight, she's a mother and grandmother working two jobs and dreaming of someday earning a college degree—somehow.

When Stacy took her break, we got out a piece of paper and worked through the BOOTS Formula. Thanks to raising kids and helping out in school offices for many years, I had some really good news for Stacy: just because she dropped out of high school didn't mean she had to start all over in order to get a college degree and find her dream job!

The best route for anyone in this situation is to go to the local community college. The counselor there can walk you through ways to take college courses or College Level Examination Program (CLEP) tests, which allow you to take exams to earn college credits. They may even be able to help you get both your general education and high school credits at the same time. Most colleges even offer *free* tutorial centers!

It may take a few extra years to catch up, particularly if you can only go part time while you're working, but each class is a step toward achieving your dreams.

Until Stacy and I talked, she thought it would be impossible to ever go to college. She promised to keep in touch and even invited me to her graduation! I'll be there with boots on.

What are some things you're not doing because someone told you they're impossible? There are always ways around things, through things, or over things. The most important thing to do is to put your boots on and start taking the first steps.

BACK TO SCHOOL...ON A BUDGET

"But Sheila," you may be thinking, "there's no way I can afford to go back to school, even if that education would help me make more money in the long run!"

To that I say, how can you afford *not* to?

Judie, the other woman at the restaurant, overheard my conversation with Stacy and confessed that she felt like it might be too late to become a flight attendant and travel the world, something she had been dreaming of since she was a little girl. She said that she'd looked into going back to school but was thinking maybe it would be wiser to just take a course in bartending to make more money.

I asked Judie, "If your daughter told you that this is what she had always wanted to do, yet she could earn an extra dollar an hour doing something that wasn't aligned with her goals, what would you tell her to do?"

She laughed, but she got serious when I followed up, "What is your happiness worth?"

The secret that most people are not aware of is that if you have lower incomes, are a single parent, and are on a budget, you can get help going back to school. You will most likely qualify for some form of grants and financial aid for books and course materials as well as class fees at the community college level.

This also works for higher education, but unfortunately the fees are higher and there are fewer grants. So higher education degrees may require shopping around at a few colleges to find one that fits your time and financial budget and gets you to the career of your choice. Don't worry so much about the name of the university; the degree and training are the important part.

If you end up needing to get a student loan, they are usually deferred at zero to very low interest while you are enrolled at least in six units. (Be sure to check this information for your specific college and state *before* signing for any loans. And please don't take on any debt if you don't need to!) Be sure to start paying back your loans *immediately*—even if it's a little each month. You're allowed to make payments on these loans even though they're not due until after you graduate. While they aren't accruing high interest, now is the time to just hack away at them a little bit at a time.

Another bonus about returning to school during a life shift is that once you start to get some of the course material in, many colleges offer work-study or paid apprentice positions. This will give you experience in a related field, which can help you get hired in your dream job.

A rock-bottom situation may be a wonderful opportunity to return to school, take up that career you always wanted to pursue, and use that increased income to pay off any high-interest debts and build your credit score. Then enjoy the gift of a new training and career, which may be the best part of whatever caused you to return to school. These days, entire industries can shift in an instant so going back to school at any age is not uncommon.

Feel free to use this affirmation that I shared with Judie (before promising to attend *her* graduation from flight-attendant school someday as well!): "I am a lifelong learner and wisdom earner!"

VOLUNTEERING

Sometimes our career shifts start as unpaid opportunities. When considering what you want to do next, you might want to think of what you'd be happy doing without even getting paid—and then go do that! Get started volunteering.

If you really want to work with animals, that might mean volunteering at the animal shelter. If you want to write, you might volunteer to write for a nonprofit. You're going to do that, and the people who may be able to give you a position in the career that you love will see you.

When you're out there giving back in contribution, they see how you connect with everybody and think, "I need someone like that. I wonder if she'd be interested in a job." The next thing you know, you're doing what you want to do. They'll see that you're not even getting paid to do this little part-time gig and understand that it's something you would love to do even if they paid you nothing.

But you're never going to get that opportunity if you're just sitting and doing the job that doesn't fit and then going home and feeling sorry about it. Instead, focus on what you truly want to be doing, what you love and care about and are good at—no matter how much (or if!) it pays.

The jobs I told you about in the Introduction—working for JPL and the phone company while I was building up my stores—were the last time I applied for a job. That's not to say I haven't worked, though.

I was given positions I never applied for because I volunteered first and they saw who I am. The next thing you know, I got the position. I've received great opportunities that led to high-paid positions as a teacher and consultant because I volunteered.

I am very passionate about equal education for all children in the United States, and I campaigned on that for many years. I have six kids and I love them all, and they deserve to have fair and equal education. I campaigned for twenty years and made some big changes in the state legislation. During that time, I volunteered and was hired as a scheduler for an assemblyman. Next thing you know, I became the campaign manager!

I've volunteered to do events, and I ended up helping with Jay Abraham's event. They saw that I could get things done and that I'm great with people.

In my first year of teacher training, I volunteered at the school. Another teacher got sick, and I was asked to take over for her even though I still had two years to go to finish my teaching degree. They didn't have anyone else, the kids loved me from being a class assistant, and so I was hired and got experience.

Be open-minded about your possibilities, then see how these opportunities lead to different places.

CAREERS SHIFT—AND SHIFT AGAIN

Career shifts happen to all of us. We don't live in a time anymore where people work for the same company their entire lives and retire from that one job. People—women especially—have to start over and reinvent themselves whenever an entire industry changes.

I never even expected that I would do the same job for my entire career and life. My passion and talents are always mine, but I know I'm going to wear different hats to apply them in my life.

You are not going to just go through a career shift once. Whether the industry changes, you get laid off, you choose to leave to follow something more closely aligned with your values, or you leave the workforce to raise children and come back after they're grown, this shift in particular happens multiple times for most women.

It takes an average of six months to a year to get to a better place and feel comfortable with how you've reorganized things around your new career. Then you're able to have more breathing room and space and you can respect what you've been through.

When you go through a career shift and come through the other side, you prove to yourself who you really are and how well you did. Then you're able to know your strength—and you don't question it anymore. You don't question yourself. You have more trust in yourself and your capabilities. It gives you that level of self-confidence because you've been through it. The next time another shift happens, you're going to be so much stronger and more prepared for it because now you have confidence. Now you know, "I did that, I got through this, and here I am. If something else hits, I'm ready. I know I got this."

If Lady's cake-decorating business had to change again, or if she hits a rock bottom in some other area of her life, she already knows that she can do it. She has a track record—and she's going to get through to the other side.

Somebody who hasn't had to deal with a rock bottom is blessed, but their muscles aren't as strong. When a rock bottom hits, it's new and scary. Whereas somebody who's built some muscles with these life shifts thinks, "Yeah, that's nothing. I got this." It's not as scary and overwhelming. You know how to apply this formula to a rock-bottom situation, and you know that—if and when you have to—you can do it again. It just needs some adjusting to whatever the particular situation is. Then it doesn't own you—you own it.

If you're facing a career change—planned or unplanned—work through the steps for whatever shift you're going through now. That will give you the confidence to know that you can go through it. But come back to it. Read this chapter again when you're leaving the workforce to retire or coming back after raising kids, or just the next time the winds of your career change direction again.

APPLYING THE BOOTS FORMULA TO CAREERS

The BOOTS Formula will help you through every career shift you make.

BEING

You're going to go through a situation or phase in your life where you're going to have to do a job or career that may not be 100 percent aligned with your life purpose, vision, or mission. You went through something. You downsized. Maybe in the moment of the shift, there's nothing in the field that is your passion. You might have to accept something that isn't exactly what you desire at that moment because you need to pay your bills.

JPL, where I used to work, went through budget cuts and thousands of employees were left without jobs. During that downturn people had to roll up their sleeves and do whatever it took to save their homes and support their families.

That doesn't mean you're stuck there; that's just reality sometimes. When that happens, you have to make the decision to show up and be the best version of yourself and give your best in whatever you're doing. Your mindset will make a difference in how you feel about waking up and going to a job that isn't 100 percent aligned with your talents. You're showing up and being in integrity.

And a lot of times when you show up in that way, you end up running into somebody who sees your integrity. The next thing you know, you're back to doing your talent because they lead you to a different job offer that's more in alignment with what fits for you. You think, "Oh wow, that's pretty cool. How did that happen?"

You know how it happened? It happened because of who you were Being. You were cleaning that store or doing data entry in that business for low pay, but you showed up and made the best you could of the situation while you're in this transition career. Because of your attitude, you became the manager. You went above and beyond for a client who made you a job offer that led you back to your industry. If you have a mission or passion or a calling or talent that you're supposed to do in life, nothing will keep you away from that for long. The opportunities will keep showing up.

I did a speaking tour and then ended up back in the little house running an Airbnb. Close to 90 percent of my guests from the speaking tour signed up for coaching with me because they were going through something. I was in a cabin up in the hill, in a tiny little isolated place, and people still felt guided to me! I never stopped helping people; it just came in a different form.

You can't remove yourself from your purpose. You just show up wherever you're placed or wherever you end up, knowing that you're going to be in this authentic essence of who you are with your unique talents. If you're a writer, you're always going to write. There are a million different things that are always going to show up if that's your biggest talent. So even if you have to humble yourself and do something that sucks and isn't your job, the right thing will align with who you're Being, and you'll be right back where you belong.

ORIENTATION

You're having a career shift or you're trying on a new career. So you're asking, "Where am I, and what do I want to do, really? How does this align with who I am?"

When I was working at JPL, I ended up teaching the safety courses and leading classes. That was a way better fit for me than programming computers. That teaching position just showed up, but I needed to be clear on what I really wanted to do long term.

Then I left and did programming for a phone company. While there, I was invited to lead the safety classes as well, and I also did some training with newly hired programmers. I was far better at leading and teaching than at sitting quietly and programming.

Listen to your body as well as your brain as you work toward finding your soul-calling. I remember that the long hours of programming meant huge chunks of time spent sitting still except for fast typing. I ended up with symptoms of carpal tunnel and didn't want to complain out of fear I would lose the benefits I so needed for my oldest son's medical issues.

Every night, I would return home to dip my hands and wrists in buckets of ice! The job was very painful because it was not aligned with my life purpose. Yes, my heart was there to make sure my son got care and the bills were paid, yet long term that field was not an option, and my body was letting me know I needed to look into something more aligned with my purpose.

If you dread going to your current job or have aches and pains all the time, it may be a gift in disguise. Listen to your body and do the inventory quiz at the end of this chapter to see if your talents are calling you into a different field. A job may pay more, but if you are paying the price in quality of life, it's not worth the cost.

ORDER OF OPERATIONS

You downsized, or you started a new career that doesn't exactly fit, and you still have a desired outcome: a better salary or a lifestyle that career would support. Obviously, you're still going to have to take small steps. If you try to do everything, you're going to get nowhere. But if you're really focused and you have your direction and your order, you will get all distractions out of your way.

You might start giving yourself one day a week to volunteer or get a part-time job or start your own business from home or whatever will support your desired outcome. It's just putting it in order to give you the most success and best results.

Once you get past the shock of the job change and start to take the next right action steps, you get out of survival mode. Then you're making progress—even if it's slow—and you're in control. A little pressure is off you, then a little more.

You may be starting over, but how can you show up and be involved in your community in another way if the job is not giving you that avenue?

THINKING

The Thinking stage is your vision for where you want to go.

Napoleon Hill tells a story in *Think and Grow Rich* about a guy who thought his way into partnership with Thomas Edison. Edwin C. Barnes decided he wanted to work *with* Edison, not *for* him. When Barnes went in to ask for the job, he had one nickel in his pocket, but he told them, "I'm going to be a partner in this company one day!"

Mr. Edison gave him the lowly job, and Barnes was there for three or four years. One day, he overheard a board meeting. Nobody believed in Mr. Edison's idea, but Barnes made a suggestion—and ended up becoming the owner's partner, as he had initially intended.

In this story, the author goes on to tell how opportunity often comes in through the side door, disguised as misfortune!

I highly recommend this book, which was one of my first life guides. When I was eight years old, things were difficult at home and I earned some money selling chocolates and helping the neighbors with chores. I went to a garage sale and purchased the book for $2.19 then ran home with it and signed my name in the front cover.

I read the book over and over again, sleeping with it under my pillow, and it helped me keep my mind laser focused on the outcomes I desired.

That focused mindset is necessary when you're going through a career shift. Let's say you're a teacher. If the school you worked in closed and you have to work as a substitute until you find a new job, you might go in to the sub job thinking, "I'm taking a pay cut and coming in as a substitute teacher. I've got to start to over." That way of thinking isn't going to get you anywhere.

But if you go in there with the attitude of, "I am going to show up like I am already a teacher at this school, and I am going to lead this class," it's going to make a difference.

You want to go in there with a positive mindset, show up, and give your best, be a blessing in this environment and put your energy toward doing the work so that people want you around—so much that they're then going to offer you a far better position than the one you left.

Your thoughts and your intention have to be that this is the result you're going to get. You have absolutely no doubt. You may not know all the steps; you just know that the next step is to start putting your foot in the door.

STEPPING UP

You have to do the work, even when it's not necessarily where you want to end up. You have to pay your bills, so you're going to do the best job you can, and it's going to lead to something better—trust me. When you apply your passion or soul-calling to whatever you're doing, your mindset shifts. People notice that. Keep Stepping Up until you're back around to being who you are. Then, when you look back, you see that you're in an even better position or with a better company or even in a better industry.

As you'll see in chapter 11 on Lifestyle Design, when you start over after a shift in your career, you can really start designing it on your own terms—and that's a beautiful thing to be able to do in life.

FROM CAREER ROCK BOTTOM TO MOMENT OF EMPOWERMENT

It was beautiful to see how the amazing women from the spa, who you read about in the beginning of this chapter, embraced their reinvention.

One woman got married after having put that part of her life on hold because she was so devoted to her work. She has a beautiful marriage that wouldn't have happened if she hadn't had the gift-in-disguise of losing that job. Another is teaching dance, using her talents in a different way—one that is even more fulfilling and self-expressive than her work at the spa.

That's the story for most of these women: it was a messy, difficult situation for a while, and now they're reorganizing and regrouping, and they're all at this better place now. It was a beautiful place and they were happy, but this fire shook things up.

Just as fire releases seeds from pine cones so new trees can grow, so did fire release these women, so they could grow in their passions. It's cool to see that life got better and they're able to have the happiness, creativity, and fun they always had.

Because they were coming from a health spa with a motivational mindset, these women were very empowered from the beginning with gratitude and knowing who they were being. And because it was an entire community, everybody supported one another. They're all close friends.

But each of those women still had to look at their own lives and see where they were starting from once they learned the spa wasn't going to open again—that was the Orientation.

Then they went into the Order of Operations, asking, "How am I going to get to what I want now?" Losing your income is a big financial shift, particularly if it's sudden. For many of the women who'd been in the same job for many years, they also lost part of their identity, their social network of colleagues and clients, and their physical location.

They thought the spa was going to reopen after the insurance fixed it, so everyone took on temporary, part-time work or got unemployment benefits to make up the lost salary until it reopened. Then the owners decided not to reopen—which was another surprise—leaving the employees to have to think quickly about more permanent next steps.

For the Thinking step, they got to see how they wanted to redesign their lives and what they want now. They looked for the gift that came from the problem.

Then they stepped into it. They're all standing strong, and they're living life more on their terms. They may not have known the words for the BOOTS Formula, but they went through the process in such a beautiful way that they're living even better than they did before.

When we have chaos in our lives and things shake us up, it's actually a beautiful way to transition to something even better. Go into your next life shift knowing that, owning it, and saying, "This is reality. How can I make this fun? How am I going to take this horrible thing and turn it into an opportunity to do life my way?"

Re-BOOT Activity: Discover Your Soul-Calling

There will be times in life where you will just need to do whatever job is in front of you in order to get back up after a rock-bottom situation. Remember that this isn't forever. As you start to reboot your life, you will once again have time to refocus. Slowly, you will be able to use your true passions and talents in order to earn a solid income. Be patient, because sometimes there are many steps between the result we desire and where we stand today.

If you are still searching for your soul-calling, you can use the following activity to get back in touch with your passion—and determine how you can make a living doing what you love!

Write down the top five things you wanted to be when you grew up.

What hobbies did you have when you were young and what hobbies would you do for free to this day? List as many as you can think of.

List what your favorite topics were when you were in school. Do these topics still interest you?

Write out a new resume and list your talents and experience. If you don't have a lot of experience yet in an area that you are naturally talented in, that's where volunteering will give you the experience and allow you to shine.

Even though you may be extremely talented in an area, employers may still require certification. Sign up for any online or in-person courses that will help you get that certificate.

If you need to return to school for a degree, that is a longer-term investment in yourself. Start building experience in the field of your dreams, even if it's for lower pay. As Tony Robbins says, "Proximity is Power!"

Check in with your circle of influence and see if any of your family or friends have connections with job openings in your field. They may be able to refer you to someone who can help you get your foot in the door. Then it's up to you to give the position your best effort!

Bonus Re-BOOT: Reboot Your Career by Owning It!

You always have the possibility of creating your own small business as an entrepreneur. This can be a great way to start something small and slowly see if it will one day create a business that affords you the opportunity to kiss your former job good-bye.

That said, when you initially start your own business, please *don't quit your day job* until you have already created other forms of passive income or you have a good six months to one year of buffer money to cover emergencies and expenses.

Here are the steps you can follow when considering your own business:

- Start by investigating your competitor! See how they market their business and what prices they charge.
- Create a business plan. I have an example on my website that is free to use, so you can create your own plan: www.SheilaMac.com/career.

- Contact your local State Board of Equalization or Better Business Bureau to find out the legal requirements for your specific city and state.
- Once you have your business plan, check into the Small Business Administration for free or low-cost personalized advice on getting your company going.
- Select your business name, and remember: You can already start doing some business in this field as a contractor, fee for service. This may be the best way to start getting income before and during the business birthing process.
- Look for online platforms that may support your business offerings and get the word out. If you want to start a driving company for famous people, start doing Uber or Lyft first to work the bugs out. If you want to start your own bed and breakfast, rent out part of your home via Airbnb.
- Be willing to actually go to work for your competitor and learn the ropes. I know this sounds interesting, but it can work very well. You will learn their systems, how they deal with customers, their cost ratio, and how satisfied are their clients. Remember that building your own business may take time, so this will get you foundational experience and training to create your own version of that business in your own area of expertise. Do not copy them; just learn the ropes.

If you are interested in starting your own business, I highly recommend that you look into two incredible programs for marketing strategies for startups. I ran my businesses prior to finding out about these programs, and I wish that I had made the investment in expert training before I had to pay the high price of learning things on my own.

I attended all of the Tony Robbins events and traveled as a Platinum Partner, learning coaching and leadership. It was an incredible experience and the best investment in my business as well as my family. To attend a Tony Robbins Business Mastery Event, check out his YouTube and Podcasts for information: https://www.tonyrobbins.com/.

You should also consider attending a Business Mastermind or training program with Jay Abraham. You can listen to his YouTube and podcasts for more business strategy methods: https://www.abraham.com/.

I had the privilege of attending a Breakthrough Mastermind at Jay Abraham's home, and the experience was as close to what I imagined a mastermind should be when reading Napoleon Hill's *Think and Grow Rich*. If you have the ability to attend one of these events, the expert advice and entire experience will help you grow a very successful business. Keep this on your bucket list and attend as your business grows, if you have the opportunity.

For more resources for finding your new career and answering your soul-calling, I have a resource section in this book, and the most current updates can be found on my website. My goal is to make sure that as you heal on your terms, you can connect to as many resources as possible.

🎁 *My Gift to You* 🎁

Dear Readers,

I am gifting you with an Individualized Career Assessment. Don't miss your chance to choose a heart centered career, where you can express your purpose, faster and easier than ever. Go to www. SheilaMacShow.com/heartwork.

CHAPTER 7

YOU'LL ALWAYS BE MY BABY (PARENTING TEENAGE AND ADULT CHILDREN)

My daughter and youngest son are only a year and a half apart, so they grew up together. They are best friends and support each other in everything—even getting into trouble together.

For her last two years of high school, my daughter and son wanted to go to a charter school I had campaigned for and helped open. The school focused on what she and her brother wanted to do for their careers. My daughter had already decided that she would study psychology. She was a straight-A student, with above a 4.0 grade point average, and a great track record. Although my son was not as decided on his major, the school and area seemed to be a great fit, so after my ex and I got divorced, we packed up our belongings and moved to a new city for a fresh start.

Whether because of starting that new school and being around different kids, stress about the move and family reorganization, peer pressure, or just teenagers making bad decisions, both of my kids got caught smoking marijuana. Worse, my daughter was driving under the influence of marijuana when they were pulled over, so a police report was filed, too.

Getting that phone call was my parenting rock bottom.

I don't drink. I don't smoke. I don't believe in using mind-altering substances. I'm aware that these things go on, but I would prefer my kids talk to me about it and not get into a car, because that's dangerous. They could have killed someone else—or themselves.

We called a family meeting, something we had done since the children were little. We went around the table and each of us had a chance to share our feelings and give input to the situation. My daughter went first, as the driver, and then my son. I asked for their side of the story. I went last and shared how scary it was as a mom to receive a call from the police.

Then I said, "You have a choice: I will pay for you to go to boarding school, and it will be a strict school because I will not have you stay in this environment. You're not making good choices, and you need more supervision than I thought. Or you can go on the Tony Robbins tour with me (traveling around the country to attend motivational seminars)."

My daughter said, "Mom, you can't afford that."

"You know what?" I replied. "I can't afford to bury you."

The kids chose to go on the tour, and that decision changed my children's entire future.

PUSHING THE BOUNDARIES

I don't care how perfect you are (or think you are!) as a parent, kids—at a certain phase—are going to test the boundaries.

When my children got in trouble, I chose to do everything I could while it was a relatively small infraction, before they did anything bigger that could risk their health, well-being, and lives. Most of the time, choices have a natural consequence in life—and those consequences will teach a lesson. It's a learning experience while the consequences are still small; they didn't crash a car, get into hard drugs, go bankrupt, or anything else that would make their lives a lot more difficult later. It's better to have those small consequences earlier, which may still hurt but which lead to personal responsibility, versus the later consequences that can be really serious—and sad.

Life is a strict teacher. It says, "If you do that, this is what's going to happen—and it's going to hurt." As a parent, you don't have to scold; you can just say, "I hope you don't do that, because I don't want to see you get hurt."

Of course, not everybody can quit their job and travel the world; I was fortunate to have a business I could run while traveling. But every parent can be present for their children as much as they are able to, while helping those children—no matter how old they are—learn to see the different options they have.

When children are younger, they need a lot of boundaries. Teenagers and young adults push those boundaries so that as they become independent adults, they can start setting boundaries of their own.

A normal, healthy part of the teenage-to-adult transition is for them to push back and say, "I want space. I want to be on my own a little more. I want to make my own decisions."

There's a dance of give and take that has to happen. As a parent, you're starting to let go. You're figuring out where those boundaries are. The level of responsibility young adults have shifts. And every month, every year, it accelerates.

I was painfully aware that, once my children turned eighteen, I couldn't make them do anything. They were going to choose what to do on their own. The best thing I could do—the best thing any parent can do—is to set them up to make decisions that give them the best possible outcomes in life…and then let them go, but be there to catch them when they fall now and then.

Parenting has a natural goal of making sure your children grow up to become productive members of society who fulfill their own talents and goals—even if that looks completely different from what you pictured for your kid. They deserve the freedom to try. Maybe that looks like not going to university right after graduating from high school. Maybe they're going to go to community college and test out different fields to see what fits best. We have to let them figure it out, so they can find their own path.

We can't control how happy they're going to be in life, how successful they'll be, or what kind of life they want to live. All we can do is model our best version of happiness, of success and of living life and let them know that we'll always be there for them. We'll always love them.

PARENTING TEENAGERS

When my youngest son was a teenager, I learned to never tell him not to do something. The minute I did, he would go do it—and he'd do it twice as much as he ever would have if I hadn't told him not to do it in the first place.

My daughter, on the other hand, would respect those boundaries and have very adult conversations with me about what was going on and why I was asking her not to do something.

Every child is different, even within the same family. And each may require a different parenting style or approach. If you treat them all the same, you may miss opportunities to nurture the unique talents that make them different. When you learn to understand and appreciate their differences, however, your children grow into independent teenagers and adults.

Here are some tips for parenting teenagers that I picked up while raising six of my own:

STEP ONE: LEARN YOUR TEENAGER'S TEMPERAMENT

Start by learning what your teenager's temperament is. It may be different from when they were a child, but one of the easiest ways to figure this out is to think back to those magical preschool days!

My first son was always interested in figuring out how his toys worked. He would break them into pieces just to see if he could put them back together again. He later became a programmer and chess player. His temperament requires contemplation; he thinks in mathematical equations, and small talk was never his thing. So to reach him, it was always best to present things using logic and science instead of feelings and emotions.

Another one of my sons has a very different temperament. He loves to be around people. I always referred to him as my hugger, and he was born laughing! He has always had a very low-key, laidback personality. He's never liked to be rushed, and as a kid he complained when I put him in too many after-school activities. He just wanted to go play at the park and have fun. He also has a photographic memory and is very smart. When he chooses to apply himself in anything, he gets the job done and nothing can stop him. I've learned that with his temperament, he's happiest choosing how he wants to best apply or not apply his talents.

My daughter is amazing and always organized (which she doesn't get from me!). She has always naturally loved structure, and if you give her a calendar or a list of things to do, she's happy. To this day, she loves order and creates her work and school schedule to ensure she is reaching her desired outcomes. When she was a young child or teen, I would write out a list and we would discuss goals together. As long as it made sense and she agreed with the schedule, she got everything accomplished.

You can also check your teenager's love language (as we covered in chapter 3, on Relationships) or use other individualized assessments. This will teach you how to express yourself as a parent so you can actually reach them, and it will show you how to talk to them and how to hear what they're saying.

STEP TWO: DETERMINE HOW YOUR TEEN RESPONDS TO THE WORLD

After you understand her temperament, determine how your child responds to the world. Although this section speaks of dealing with a teen, it relates to older and younger children's personalities as well.

During the teen years, a child is going through a lot of transitions, both physically with hormones as well as emotionally. They are experiencing the growing pains of first loves and learning how to fit in with peers in school, the pressures of school and getting good grades, and the reality of preparing to leave home to go off to college or start a career. It's a scary time of rapid growth as a child begins to develop their identity and autonomy.

With that being said, how your child reacted when younger is going to be very different during these teen years.

How does your child respond when they are happy? When overwhelmed? When things don't go right and they get bad news or are dealing with drama at school? Your teenager may act out, or respond with anger, or seclude themselves in their room. The question to be aware of is at what point is their response something to be concerned about?

If you start to feel uncertain about where your child is headed, it may be helpful to have a "pre-discussion" about consequences. Creating a family meeting, even at this stage and age, can make a huge difference. It may even be necessary to help them reboot, which we'll talk about in just a moment, in step four.

STEP THREE: DISCOVER HOW YOUR TEENAGER LEARNS BEST

Third, discover how they learn best.

We all learn differently. Some people do well listening in class and can remember just about everything they hear. Others have verbal processing issues and need to read to get their best results. There are those who are often seen taking voracious notes; they tend to be more kinesthetic in nature, and the feeling of the act of writing itself helps their minds remember more about the topic. Some must repeat or verbally speak something to memorize it deeply.

Because I was both a Montessori and Waldorf teacher over the years, I got to study how to reach children using many different modalities. It helped me to understand how to reach my own teens better as well as how to learn and continue to educate myself.

When you determine the strongest way to support your teenager's learning, you can be sure that what you're saying—or writing—sticks.

STEP FOUR: TEACH YOUR CHILDREN THE BOOTS FORMULA

The last step is to teach your children the BOOTS Formula, so they can use it through their own inevitable ups and downs.

Having smaller rock-bottom moments when they're younger helps your children learn to move through them and hopefully helps prevent hitting too many more rock bottoms as they grow into adulthood.

When you share some of the small steps you take while going through a tough situation or even a rock bottom, you are teaching your children to be prepared and successful adults. We all have our waves in life, and the best thing we can do as parents is give our children the tools to be able to handle any situation that may show up.

- Ask your child who they are *Being* during their struggles at school (or elsewhere) and how they need to show up in order to modify the situation.
- Help them assess their *Orientation:* Where are they with their homework assignments, for example, and where do they need to be to get the grades they want?
- Help them to think through the *Order of Operations* (a nice way to introduce a higher math concept early on): What would be the best first step to take? Once they've taken that first action, what is the next logical step?
- Then remind your teen about how their *Thinking* can help

them with their life. What mindset will best help them in this situation?

- Finally, help them to learn how to set goals and *Step Up* and take action toward their own desired outcomes. It may be that they want to have friends over for a party. Together, you could write out a few steps and make an agreement that if they do these action steps, you'll let them have their party.

I have a different relationship with each of my children because I know what their temperament is, I know how they respond, I know how they learn, and I know they have the tools they need to think and plan through difficult life situations. Where one may have needed more space as a teenager, another needed firmer boundaries, and yet another needed additional guidance because they were still an immature young adult.

With these steps established, you and your teenagers will have better communication. When they have an issue, they will be less likely to hide it. They can come to you before it gets really bad. They'll feel safe in your relationship, so they can tell you the shift that's happening in their life before they hit rock bottom. Then you can talk through it, help them reboot if necessary, and they'll be a lot more open to your parenting.

KNOW THEM AND KNOW THEIR FRIENDS

One of the most important things Tony Robbins says is, "We're the direct reflection of our peer group."

If we see our kids get into the wrong peer group, the best thing to do is make some kind of a shift. That may mean moving, sending them to a different school, or having them go to a summer program.

Maybe you can't afford to move or pay for pricy summer camps. That's okay. It just needs to be enough of a shift to shake up their perspective. Connect them with Girl Scouts, Boy Scouts, community service, or an after-school activity they love, maybe a dance class, sports team, or arts program. It may mean getting them involved in some different classes to occupy their time and connect them with a more solid group.

That way, your teenager is connecting with kids who are actually doing things your child wants to do anyway. It's not taking them out of their social life but taking them out of a group that may be going down the wrong road. Then they can see that they don't have to do what "everybody else" is doing, which may be the wrong choice. Instead, the people around them will be applying themselves and working toward finding their talents.

As important as a peer group is for a teen, or even for adults, it all boils down to personal responsibility. The moment a teen or parent stops blaming the others and focuses on new solutions is the moment a person is truly free. It seems hard to do, yet as a parent, modeling this type of responsibility can actually be the best training tool.

If you have a teen at home, it may be helpful to point out your own teen or young adult experience. You may want to share how, when you were a young adult, once you were able to own your role in the situation, the problems disappeared and the solutions appeared. Once a teen applies this concept, it is so empowering, and they can use it as a tool for future difficult situations, in college or in the business world.

PARENTING ADULT CHILDREN

My children are all legally adults now, but I am always going to be their mom—and sometimes I still want to parent them.

As we've discussed, there's a transition from child to teen, teen to young adult, and from young adult to fully fledged adult. Your relationship with your children will reinvent itself over the years. The responsibility shifts, the dialogue changes, you talk about things more openly—or create stronger boundaries around the subjects you don't want to talk about. You're still a parent but you shift to an advisor or friend role, someone they can come to and confide in about what's going on in their lives. You become a guide instead of someone who tells them what to do.

You're not going to agree with everything your adult children do. And that's okay. Not everybody agrees with what I do. We all have our own decisions to make. But what if they keep making what you consider stupid choices, even as adults?

Sometimes you just have to have the attitude of, "I'm not going to say anything. I don't agree with this particular decision, but I love this person." Or even acknowledge, "I don't agree with this, but if you're going to do it anyway, that's your choice."

You agree to disagree. You choose your battles. But sometimes a boundary is crossed and you, as a family, have to decide how to deal with that in the most loving way possible. You'll always love your children, but they don't live under your roof, so you can decide how you want them in your life. This may sound harsh, but it's real and your grown children will appreciate receiving honesty with love over having to lie to your face about how they are living their lives.

Some families choose not to discuss certain things openly, and others share just about everything—each family unit has to decide on their own limits.

I've heard of parents disowning their grown children over who they choose to date, or something as simple as a young adult changing their hair color or getting a piercing or tattoo. While that may not have been a parent's goal or ideal for their child, if you think back to your own teen or young adult years, there were always ways of expressing yourself, and those generational expressions change over time.

Don't throw your adult baby out with the bathwater of the times. They are now adults and may decide to make changes later. Most will settle into their own less extremes once they test the boundaries and limits and are ready to settle down and get serious about careers or starting their own families.

As much as possible, see where you can meet in the middle, as adults.

You're going to love your children no matter what. And you'll like the good parts about them. You don't have to like the parts that don't align with your values or your vision for them—that's their life. They own it now.

A SAFE SPACE

Just like with teenagers, if you honor who your adult children are and who they're showing up as—even though you might not agree with a large portion of what they're doing at the moment—it makes you a safe place for them to come to.

But if you treat an adult like a child, you are most likely to be met with dishonesty, distance, pushback, and resentment.

If every time you get together you go in circles about a lifestyle choice—because you don't like their job or boyfriend or girlfriend—they're not going to want to come over and visit or share real things with you. Is it worth doing that to your relationship? Don't waste your constantly shrinking, precious time on things you can't change.

How many people on this planet have to go home to their family on Thanksgiving or Christmas and think, "Ugh, this is hell. I don't want to go because these people are going to throw all their opinions on me, and I don't want to hear any of it."

The holidays become a painful obligation. I don't know about you, but I don't want to be a painful obligation.

Instead, try to focus on all the good: the things you align on, the moments spent laughing and having fun, talking about your shared history, and making new memories. Do whatever makes you all happy this year, during this season of your life. It doesn't have to be what you've always done, where everybody gets the hell out as fast as they can because they don't want to be there.

For example, as a family, we decided to celebrate our holidays differently. We have our own traditions, and my kids bring their significant others and children into the mix.

One year, after spending a small fortune and three long days preparing the Thanksgiving meal and doing all the decorations—while running a business and taking care of elder family members—everybody showed up having already eaten one or two meals at other houses they'd had to "stop by" on the way to my house. They were too stuffed to eat all the food I had so carefully cooked!

That day, I announced that for future Thanksgivings I was going to gift myself a trip to a wellness spa for a few days over the course of my birthday! I would rather spend that time and money on wellness, and we could plan to do a healthy, fun family activity that focused less on food and more on connection.

One time we toured Catalina Island. Another time, we rented bikes and rode them on Venice beach. Sometimes we have a slumber party at my house with pillow fights like when they were kids. Now my adult children come over and visit because they actually *want* to. As an adult with adult children, I get to be a kid again and play with them and have fun. We're building magic memories. And that's what they're going to remember for the rest of their lives.

STRIKE A BALANCE

No matter how old your children are, it's important to strike a balance in how much help you give them.

As young children, we all need a lot of help figuring out the world around us. As we get older, we need less help learning to walk and talk, read and write, ride our bikes or throw a ball, and more help navigating the complicated world of adults. Whether your children are teenagers or adults, it's necessary to adjust your level of involvement in order to maintain that balance.

DON'T OVER-HELP

When you over-help, giving your children too much and not asking that they take any personal responsibility, they may start to believe that they can't do anything for themselves. They've never had to prove themselves and use their talents to produce something. They haven't had to become a functioning adult.

When I was a teacher, there were always those parents who did their children's class projects for them. It was pretty clear when the eight-year-old walked in with a working rocket ship model that he didn't make it himself. But the kid who came in with this funny-looking project that they put their heart and soul into deserved an A because I could see they did it themselves.

There's a treatment program called Failure to Launch for adult children who have never left home. For whatever reason, they are unable to gain the independence they need to live their own lives. These parents pay thousands of dollars to get their child the help they need in order to grow up.

That's a lot of money. It's far more affordable to do something that makes a bigger difference when they're younger.

As you watch your child and think, "Damn, that's not what I'd do," there's this inclination to say, "Let me help you." But if you're able to step back and give them space while still saying, "I'm your parent, and I'm always here for you. If you need something, I'm going to show up. If something happens, you've always got a place. But I want you to fly, and I want you to make those choices," it helps them develop confidence.

A young adult grows by figuring out how to get a job, make their own money, and have some responsibilities. You'll have a much healthier, happier kid that way than if you give them everything and they never get to learn the responsibility of becoming an adult.

After she came back from the Tony Robbins tour, my daughter got a job managing a Starbucks while she went to school. One day, she came over and said, "See that red car over there? I bought it!"

She was so proud—and I'm proud of her, too. She makes the payments and takes care of the maintenance on the car. She's able to appreciate the car more than she would have if I had bought it for her. And it's beautiful to see the self-confidence that came from figuring it out herself.

BUT DON'T UNDER-HELP EITHER

Over time, you and your children will get to a really solid place where they start having more self-respect and self-confidence and you can step back from helping more and more.

But you don't want to step back *too* far; you don't want to under-help. You want to be there as a safety net to a certain extent. Your children should know that if they get sick or have an emergency, they have their parents to turn to for support.

You're letting go of the apron strings with lots of love—and logic.

This concept works like the honor system—you give them a little bit of freedom, and if they step too far and fall, you're going to pull back. For example, if you leave them home alone and they have a party, your child is going to have to re-earn your trust—and they certainly won't be able to stay home alone again for a while.

You know your unique, individual child and what they can handle better than anyone, but you'll need to have open and honest conversations with them as well. Ask them, "How much do you think you can handle?" and then trust your gut. It's better to give freedoms a little bit at a time and let your child earn the next step, so you may want to suggest a trial basis for so many weeks or months before going on. You can always pull back if necessary, and eventually let them earn it again.

Ask your child, "What are you showing me? That you can be responsible or can't?" Having an honest, open discussion will help this young adult be more receptive than talking down to them. Finally, keep any teachers and other adult family members in the discussion, so that you are all working together on the same, honest page.

YOU ARE SOMEBODY'S CHILD, TOO

So far, we've talked about your relationship as a parent to a child, but it's important to remember that you are also somebody's child. What is your relationship like with your parents?

As an adult child yourself, you play an important role in the relationship you have with your parents—and you play an important role in changing that relationship as well.

At some point—depending on your age, that time may have been relatively recent or farther in the past—you, too, wanted to grow up, have your own space, and become independent. You had to navigate, or are still navigating, how to be both your parents' child—no matter how old you are, you'll always be their kid—*and* an adult.

We do a dance with our parents (and our children, just from the other side). They tend to fall into the pattern of parenting, and we may regress into acting like children. Have you ever caught yourself rolling your eyes—you, a grown-up adult!—as you said, "Okayyyy, Mom!"? You would never act that way with other adults, but it's normal to fall back into these familiar roles of parent and child.

Just as you'll always be their child, your parents will always be your parents. But as an adult, you can move toward having a friendship with them, too. You can start to see your parents for who *they* are—not just providers, but people. You can build a bond on an adult level, which is so much deeper and better because you're changing those roles.

You may feel guilty when your parents accuse you of not calling or visiting enough. Or you may feel they are still somehow controlling and running your life. You may feel smothered by their constant intrusions and over-involvement in your adult life. But none of these is the real problem. You don't have a mom who won't let you go or a mom who makes you feel guilty. The real issue is that you have a personal character problem: You need to develop your identity and autonomy and learn how to set boundaries.

So how can you change that relationship? By changing the steps in the dance.

Remember when you used to try on your mom's heels as a child? Well, it's time to step into her shoes again. Try to consider your mom's perspective: you were once her baby. She was devoted to taking care of you for your entire life, and now she feels like you're pushing her away. You left home, and she felt alone. She may feel like she's losing an important part of her identity or going through empty-nest syndrome. One of my friends described it as, "I just got fired as a mom."

Understanding that perspective is the first step in making a switch. Then ask yourself, "How can I fulfill my mother's need to mother me and love me, yet have my own independence?"

Maybe that means calling her every week or sending a voice message instead of texting, so she can hear your voice. Maybe it's sending a card and flowers for special occasions—or just to say you're thinking of her. It may be that you simply send love to help her fill that void.

While sending your mom (or both parents) love, make sure that you're also establishing a new pattern. Set healthy boundaries for yourself. Remind her that you love her—but you can't talk on the phone for an hour every day. Your parents will always want to protect you, but you're not a baby. You have to fall down and get up and learn your own lessons. Let them know you're safe, but don't feel like you have to explain yourself or answer to them. Give them whatever information you're comfortable sharing, even if it's limited, and give it with love and understanding.

Finally, reaffirm your relationship and remind your parents that you're still their child, and you'll always be there for them too; your relationship is just going to take on a different form.

I have a friend who didn't date for years because she was raising her daughter. Now her daughter is grown, and my friend feels like she's being pushed away. We were talking one day, and she asked, "Can I let her go?"

I paused and asked her, "Can you hold her back?"

My friend's daughter *wants* her mom to let go. She wants to change that relationship. And she wants her mom to know that she doesn't have to always *act like* a mom. Now, they can be friends and have each other's back.

APPLYING THE BOOTS FORMULA TO PARENTING

Parenting is an important role because your actions affect yourself and at least one other person. The BOOTS Formula can help you *and* your child be the best you can be.

BEING

Who are you Being with your children? How are you modeling how to show up during difficult situations?

As a teacher, I would often see parents who would come into a conference complaining about how their child does things a certain way, and it really bothered them. The child was usually reenacting what the parents modeled. For instance, the parents who yelled in the parking lot, in front of their children, were often the ones who complained about their child shouting.

So, pay attention to how you are Being and think about ways to honestly model the steps you take to stay centered and grounded during difficult situations.

ORIENTATION

Your children are not better than they are or worse than they are—they are simply *who* they are. Get to know your teenagers and adult children for who they are, as they are right now. Be honest. Own everything that makes them who they are—but keep them accountable for who they want to be.

The terrible twos are the first signs of independence. Our little ones start to say no and defy adults. They are at the beginning stages of learning about their autonomy. Later, in the teen years, you will find that one day your teen wants to be hugged and cared for and the next they are angry that you're telling them what to do and not giving them more freedoms. Eventually, when your young adult leaves home and ventures off into their own school or career, they are going to decide how to express themselves.

Each parent has a unique understanding of their child, as well as a mother's or father's intuition. Trust your gut on parenting. If you feel that something is really off, like your son or daughter is not acting the same, seems depressed, or is going through something more serious than they let on, *believe* that feeling. Do your best to talk openly with your teen or young adult about where they really are and where they want to be.

It helps to start this process of open communication with your children when they are young, but it is never too late to learn how to have honest conversations.

ORDER OF OPERATIONS

Once you know what the situation really is, it may be wise to call a meeting between parents, grandparents, teachers and any other adults who work closely with your child or teen. It's up to you to decide how much information you will share with them, but if you can discuss what is in the best interest of your young one, together you will be able to come up with an aligned action plan. Then, when you present this for open discussion with your child or young adult, you can all agree on the best Order of Operations.

I have done this with my own young adults and helped other parents with this process. There is a sense of ownership that comes when a young adult gets to bring their input and feedback into the mix—and relief when they know they have an aligned support group to help them get back on track. Yes, you may still get some pushback initially, yet if you are able to address this as a parent, putting love and logic in place rather than emotion, your entire family will benefit.

THINKING

What mindset do you have as a parent? What is your vision for how your relationship looks, now and in the future?

There is a point in every parent's life where we lose our identity or role as a parent. Our children are now teens or adults, and they are fighting for their freedom. At first, this can feel happy yet sad at the same time. Your mindset and Thinking are really important here. Thank yourself for raising your child well; the fact that they want to express themselves and think for themselves means you have done your job very well.

Your role now changes a bit, and you slowly move from parenting a child to advising a young adult. It is here that keeping your Thinking on the positive will help. What a teen or young adult does when they are "finding themselves" and expressing their autonomy is not going to be where they end up as they continue to develop and grow. So choose your battles and remember that what you focus on grows. Instead of thinking about and focusing on the parts that you may not fully align with, give real reinforcement, compliments, and support to their victories.

STEPPING UP

Step into that relationship you envisioned! Set a new standard for how you communicate with your young adult or adult child, perhaps being more open about aspects of higher education and adult life. You may want to step up with vulnerability here and share some stories about your young adult experiences, especially how you felt, the emotions you went through, and perhaps the learnings you had to make on your own. This gives your young adult the opportunity to feel safe sharing things that they may be going through or that they will also experience in their own way and time.

FROM PARENTING ROCK BOTTOM TO MOMENT OF EMPOWERMENT

When I got the call from the police that the kids had been pulled over, my hand was glued to my phone with sweat. I could barely breathe as the voice on the other end of the phone said that a parent had to come get the car.

I drove home slowly with the windows rolled down, airing out the marijuana smell and allowing my head to clear a bit. I didn't know whether to laugh or cry, I was so upset at what they had done and so relieved that they hadn't hurt anyone.

In that moment, I had to decide who I was going to be as a parent.

I had to ask myself, "How am I going to show up?" Was I going to yell and scream at my kids? No, that would just push them away. Instead, I chose to talk with them from a very honest place. I talked to my kids like the young adults they were—not scolding them or talking down to them—and said, "Hey, we just moved here. This is what I'm seeing, and I'm not happy with it, so there are going to be consequences. But I want you to know that I love you and want what's best for you."

Everybody was a teenager at some point in their lives. Who doesn't have a story of some stupid, crazy thing you did as a kid or teenager because the other kids were doing it? It's a rite of passage we all go through. My kids had a legal consequence— they were placed on probation and later had to appear before the court with an explanation of what they had been doing to change their ways (and you'll see in just a minute that they had a great experience to share). That may have been enough, but I wanted to go a little farther as a parent to really instill the consequences—but in a loving way.

This rock bottom was a gift in disguise. Often, a difficult situation forces us to take massive action, step out of our comfort zones, and do whatever it takes to produce different—and better—results.

It was incredibly difficult to take the emotion out of making that decision, but I didn't want to come from a place of anger and hurt. It wasn't, "I'm going to sell your car because you did something wrong with it." It was, "I'm going to sell your car and use that money toward giving you a life-changing experience because I love you."

I wasn't going to make it worse than it was, and I wasn't going to make it better than it was. I just had to deal with it as it was. I had to decide what options to give them, and they were: go to boarding school because there wasn't enough supervision and my kids weren't at the level of maturity I'd thought, or come with me and go on the tour. I really wanted them to choose the tour because I had already planned to go while they stayed with their dad, but I still wanted them close to me as much as possible—but I gave them the choice.

Once they made that choice, I followed my Order of Operations: we sold the car, talked to the right people to get them booked on the tour, signed them up for an independent study program so they could do home schooling while we traveled, and created a lesson plan. It took less than a week, and then we were on tour.

The Thinking step was putting the vision of what they were going to get out of this program in their minds, thinking of how to make this a fun learning experience—and how to work together while traveling on a budget and having to share hotel rooms.

I was on the tour for seven years, and they were there with me for the first two of those years. The tour was a safe space for my children to finish growing up, surrounded by people who are all about personal development.

Their first event we did was business mastery, where you create a pretend business and then advertise and market that business. You talk about how your business is going to be socially responsible, how it gives back. And all the teams compete to see how their business would do in the real world.

Well, my children grew up with a mom who had a business. But they were still teenagers, so at first their attitude was that they were just in trouble and only there because they were being punished. A twenty-three-year-old in their group said, "Hey, what's up with the attitude? You've got to fix that."

My daughter told me about what he'd said and added, "Mom, he just acts like he's the shit."

Then they found out that if your team loses, you have to go on stage and explain why the business you created failed. They said, "Oh, no. We're not going to be losers." And they started playing the game. My daughter stayed up all night making posters and T-shirts while my son thought up a marketing campaign.

The next day, that young guy got on stage, and it turned out he's a multibillionaire in internet marketing. My daughter came up to me and said, "Mom, he *is* the shit!"

There was a big shift after that. She recognized that maybe he did have something to say—and that was why I was investing in my children. On the tour, they got to see people who have decided to use their creativity to be resourceful, create a business, and have success. It was a beautiful gift to my children at the teenage phase where they're testing boundaries and figuring out their own identities as they go through the shift from child to adult.

Even after the tour, my children stepped up. My daughter

brought over a friend who was cutting so we could have an intervention with his parents. She helped another friend who had an eating disorder. She became a leader, and so did my son. They had perspective, so they could talk their peers through making the right decisions—while understanding that they get to choose, too. You can't force them to change, because sometimes they don't; you just love them.

I had to step up and step back at the same time, to trust them to step into the kind of adults I was preparing them to be. And then they stepped up themselves, in turn, because of everything we had set in motion together.

My son's favorite experience on the Tony Robbins tour was hearing a man named Keith Cunningham speak about accounting and business finances, which he explains through a sports metaphor. My son—who's always been super smart and great at everything—heard that and he said, "I love accounting. That's what I want to do!"

He's now majoring in accounting in college—all from that first event; it made such an impression on him.

My daughter was able to do a mentorship with Cloé Madanes even though she wasn't quite eighteen yet. Cloé Madanes is a leader in psychology today; if you get your master's degree in psychology, you have to study her work. My daughter was already interested in psychology, but she totally resonated with Cloé—and that connection is what she was looking for.

Now, she's majoring in psychology. She's a junior counselor at a girls' home called St. Ann's that helps teenage mothers in the foster care system. Her time with Cloé put her on a great path and set her up for success—not just with the academic skills we learn in school but also the real-world skills that are necessary for the rest of life.

I gave my children the best options I could. I asked them, "Do you want to study Cloé Madanes' work, or do you want to sit in her classroom and have a discussion with her? Do you want to read about Steve Forbes, or do you want him to be speaking in front of you?"

I think they made the right choice.

Re-BOOT Activity: Parent/Child Relationship Agreement

It's time to get off the battlefield and back to love! One way to do this is to create a parent/child relationship agreement. These can be written or verbalized. Below are some examples to help you create your own unique agreement.

Dear Son or Daughter,

I am so happy to see you become an adult in both age and maturity. I know that sometimes you still will want parental advice, but sometimes I will accidentally start doing what I have done for the last eighteen years. So, let's agree that if I overstep or forget your boundary in this area that you just use the code word _____ and I'll stop immediately, no pushback.

As two adults, there are some things that we are just not going to completely agree on. I have raised you with my values and beliefs; you know what those are by now. There are things that you may wish to refrain from sharing with me, or that I may not want to know about. I will always love you, and I understand that you are going to do as an adult does, and at times you may end up down a road that is not such a good fit. Just know that we can agree to disagree, and if you feel a need to share about one adult situation or another, we can talk. If I am not up for that discussion, I will let you know.

And the same goes for you; our love and respect for each other will continue to grow even if we do not always align on life choices. I ask that you be as honest with me as you feel is possible. If you want advice, you always know I am here to give it or just a loving listening ear.

I promise to tell you the full truth, even when it's sometimes scary to do so. As the years go by, our roles may change, and as much as I appreciate your truth, there may be times where you will need to hear mine.

I agree to put effort into learning how you most like to be listened to, and then listen to you in that way as often as I can.

I agree to love and support you when you need it, to lovingly push and encourage you when you need it, and to honor your space if that is what you need.

I agree to make myself as emotionally complete as possible in my own life, so that I can show up as my best self for our adult parent to adult child relationship.

I agree to be aware of, and own, my own emotional triggers and ask you to do the same.

I agree to not waste precious time or energy on the blame game. Let's just discuss solutions and strategies as two adults.

And above all else, I promise to love and respect you.

Sincerely,

Mom (or Dad)

Depending on what state you live in and the financial costs of living independently, it is not unheard of for adult children to return home for a short time after college or in order to reboot their own lives after a rock-bottom event. If you find yourself in that situation with your child, this agreement may help you both live in harmony!

Rental or Room and Board Agreement

_____ (parent), _____ (parent), and _____ (adult child)

While _____ (name of adult child) is living in our/my home, _____ (amount of rent) will be due weekly or monthly, on _____ (date or day of the week).

This rent will cover housing, food, electricity, heat/AC, water, cable television, and/or internet access. Extra chores may be negotiated in lieu of rent, if agreeable to both parties.

Mutual respect for everyone who resides here, as well as for the neighbors, is required. Friends are not permitted to spend the night, and advanced notice on those we do not already know are required for day visits at the home, as we also live here and prefer our privacy.

All persons will refrain from cursing, name-calling, intimidation, and/or threats while living in the household.

_____   _____

Parent(s) signature(s)   Signature of adult child/tenant

If you're looking for additional resources for parenting adults, I have a resource section in this book, and the most current updates can be found on my website. My goal is to make sure that as you grow your new parenting relationship, on your terms, that I connect you to as many resources as possible. I also have additional activities for you to strengthen your relationship to an adult child or as an adult to your parent.

🎁 *My Gift to You* 🎁

Dear Readers,

For years I had other people telling me that to be an outstanding parent I must be very rigid in how I parent my teenage and adult children. When I realized that was not true, I was finally able to break old parenting patterns, open lines of communication with my children, and create the relationship I truly desired with my young adult children.

To get the **5 *Secrets to Success to Parenting your Teen or Young Adult with Love and Logic*** go to: www.SheilaMac.com/parentadults.

....

CHAPTER 8

....

PARENTING YOUR PARENTS (ELDERCARE)

I'm a member of what they call "the sandwich generation," women who care for their parents and their children at the same time. In my case, though, it was more like a full-course meal: I took care of both sets of grandparents, my parents, and my children.

My mom and dad both had serious health issues at the same time that my grandparents on both sides were also having trouble. I ran around visiting relatives in three different hospitals and a rehabilitation center. Plus, I was running my four gift stores—and pregnant, with all the extra emotions that come with that.

I was only in my mid-twenties, the only child and grandchild, so I had nobody to take over visiting one hospital after the other, or to help figure out how to care for all these people. This was *so much* to take on. To be the sole decision-maker for all these family members, the only one to meet with doctors, to consider

PARENTING YOUR PARENTS (ELDERCARE) · 211

every option and understand every treatment…I wanted to run to my parents or grandparents and say, "Hey, give me some advice! I'm still young. How do I deal with all this?"

Neither of my grandparents, on either side, wanted to leave their homes and go into a nursing home. When they got closer to the end of their lives, though, they had to be hospitalized. The doctor wanted them to go into a rehabilitation center, but they refused. I offered to have them come stay with me, so I could take care of them in my home. They didn't like each other, though, so they didn't want to live together.

They just wanted to go home—but I couldn't pay for four people to have the round-the-clock care they needed.

We were all stuck at rock bottom together.

THE ROLES CHANGE AGAIN

This chapter is the opposite of the previous. Instead of talking about parenting your adult child, we're now going to look at the flip side: having to become a parent figure for your elderly parents, once they're not able to fully take care of themselves anymore.

You used to be the child—even as you're an adult—and now you have to become the parent in the relationship. You're used to having your parents be the solid rock in your life, turning to them for advice and support, and now you're responsible for making decisions about their life. The roles you have with your parent have to be turned upside down.

There may be pushback from your parents, whose roles are

changing too. Who the hell are you to check up on them and tell them to take their medications? But if you have built that deeper, stronger relationship discussed in chapter 7, it will make that transition to caring for your parent easier because you have healthy boundaries and are on closer terms.

DON'T TREAT YOUR PARENT LIKE A CHILD

Even though you're an adult with the responsibility of parenting a parent, if you treat your parent like a child, you're going to get the same results as with a child. They'll become resentful if you push them to do what you think is best without respecting what they want.

Let's say you—and your siblings or other relatives, if you have them—have decided to sell your parents' house, because they're no longer able to live alone. You look at it as making it easier on your family to help take care of them, but they don't want anything to do with it. It's *their* house, and that's where they're staying.

They're adults. They're used to taking care of themselves. They probably still think they've got it all under control—even though they might not have any control at all anymore. They don't want you to tell them what to do; they have to come to it themselves.

You're going to continue getting that pushback unless you can honor them and plant the seeds of the idea, until your encouragement leads your parent to come to that conclusion on their own. You can give them other resources and ways of looking at the situation so that instead of coming from you as a command, you're guiding them to that place.

This could be as simple as asking doctors, or wellness care facilities to explain the process, allowing your parent to ask questions, going on tours, and involving them in exploring their options. There is something magical about not forcing anything yet allowing your parent to discover the options and choose what is best for them.

You may be able to interview other peers who have faced similar transitions and who are really happy about their choice. It would be even better if you found a person who initially questioned or fought this choice, for fear of losing their freedom and autonomy, who now finds it to be the best decision they ever made. If you Google these options, you'll find many interviews and stories that you can share with your parent.

When it's their choice—just like with your children—you support their options. They get the buy-in of the outcome, the results of making that choice, and then you're not forcing it. They're like, "Let's go! I'm packing my bag."

You're there to support them and honor what they choose to do.

This is a tough time. They are going through something too—something that may be their own rock bottom, which they may or may not come out of. It may mean a very different lifestyle and quality of life.

Things are already hard for your parents. Having to make this huge shift can lead to feeling a loss of control and autonomy. You don't want to make their life any harder than it has to be. Allowing your parents to maintain some personal responsibility gives them self-esteem and a sense of purpose and meaning. You are giving them that empowerment, that sense of owning their life and their decisions. Once they own it, it's so much easier than you pushing it on them.

SIBLING RIVALRY

You may have brothers and sisters or other family members who have their own feelings about the decision of what to do for your parent. Eldercare can become a conflict of the heart, which may then turn into a sibling rivalry.

If you have siblings who are also involved with your parent as co-trustees or caregivers, you all want the best possible wellness routine, living situation, or choice for that person—but you may all have vastly different ideas of what that looks like. When each person feels like their idea is the most informed decision, war often breaks out on the home front.

When this happens, it may become necessary to get a third party involved. This could start with having a family friend, religious or community leader, or in some cases a mediator or court get involved in resolving this sort of conflict.

The ideal situation, though, is to work together as a team for the common goal of honoring your parents and giving them their wishes; this makes it so much easier for everybody.

One of my clients, Irma, had to work very hard to get to this place with her family.

Irma is in her late sixties, but she is still considered the baby in her family—even though she has grown children and three grandchildren of her own! Her older siblings talked down to her, disrespected her, and treated her like a child.

Her parents also treated her like a baby—while simultaneously leaning heavily on Irma and her husband financially. When Irma's dad had heart surgery, none of her siblings had the money to help out, so she and her husband paid for all the extra expenses. When Irma's mom wanted to take that lifelong dream vacation to Ireland, Irma paid for the whole family to go.

As her parents got older and needed more care—and, therefore, more help with those expenses—it was time for Irma to have some difficult discussions.

She and her husband sat down with her siblings and explained how overextended their parents were and how much they needed to avoid a financial crisis. Irma had decided ahead of time to coordinate a family pool, contributing her fair portion toward helping her parents, but she needed help coming up with additional options and supporting her parents through some tough choices.

When their siblings saw just how much Irma and her husband were contributing—and how well she pulled together a plan to help their parents further—they started to show her more respect.

Irma and her siblings presented the available options to their parents, who ultimately decided to sell their house and move to a senior community in California called Leisure World. This gave her parents the buffer they needed and gave Irma and her husband their own space to build a nest egg without feeling the financial burden of bailing out her parents.

Most importantly, Irma's parents were able to make an empowering decision about their own future and all the siblings saw how strong they could be when they supported each other.

DECISION TIME

Sooner or later, you may become the person responsible for advocating for healthcare, respecting your elderly parents' wishes, and making all of the difficult decisions that come with eldercare. Here are some questions to think about and tips to help guide you when the time comes:

WHERE TO LIVE

At some point, your parents may have to leave the house they call home. Maintaining the same level of independent living they did previously may become too hard, unless they are able to have a full-time staff to help. And there are a lot of decisions that have to be made when the time comes.

Will they go into a rehabilitation center, senior housing, or nursing home, or will they live with you or another relative? How are you going to provide for their needs? How are you going to pay for it? A lot of the cost is not covered by insurance—so it has to come out of somebody's budget. Are you going to be able to keep their house, or will you rent it out or sell it?

This is a big decision. People are tied to where they live. Because you don't want to take away your parents' agency if you don't have to, you may consider asking, "At this point, is your house serving you or are you serving your house?" This gives them the option of participating in the choice. It's their life, and this is where they're going to live, so it's best to let them choose.

I know an older woman who is absolutely devoted to animals. She spent much of her life rescuing greyhounds from the racetrack. She made it clear that when she passed away, she wanted to donate everything to an animal society.

But she didn't have to wait until she died to make a difference.

Ultimately, with the help of her family, she decided to change her living situation, selling her house and moving into a senior center. She realized that with the money she saved on upkeep for a big house with only one person living in it, she had more to give to the animals. Her empty house didn't give her the same level of happiness she got from snuggling baby kittens.

That decision totally extended her life, she enjoyed every moment of it, and of course the animals were absolutely blessed.

QUALITY OF LIFE

Maybe your parents aren't sick, but they're getting older. They could live so much better if they downsized their living situation and were able to travel to see their children or take care of their health better to give them greater longevity.

Quality of life is an important factor to consider—at any age or stage of life. There comes a point where you have to ask, "Hey, how many years do we have left?" (Although you also have to accept never quite knowing the answer.) Celebrate this life now. Do everything you can to give your parents the best quality of life.

A big part of quality of life is mindset. Instead of looking at it as having to make big, life-altering, scary changes, try to help them see the positives. It's a lot easier to say, "You have to change your lifestyle, but now you get to do all these things you've always dreamed about, that make you happy in life," than, "The doctor says you have to move and we have to sell your house because we can't afford it."

Maybe there's a health situation, so your parents are limited in their options of where to live. But if they were lonely in the house by themselves, moving somewhere with more people who are at the same stage can lead to a better quality of life.

If your parents have friends or people in the same age range who are facing similar decisions, get a few of them together to go look at retirement communities so it's not as scary as going alone. Instead of suffering alone at home, or worrying about not knowing anyone, it will ease the transition as they meet new people, get more comfortable, and discover how happy they can be when all their needs are easily met.

MEDICAL DECISIONS

You may end up being the medical and health conservator or trustee for your parents. This means that they grant you the responsibility of overseeing their healthcare and wellness choices based on a preset form that describes their wishes. In the resources section of my website, at www.SheilaMac.com/elders, you will find additional information about becoming a healthcare advocate.

Sometimes an adult parent is going to choose a different treatment or living option than you want. At what point should you step in if your parent makes a decision that goes against your beliefs as to what's best for their health or safety?

The reality is that as long as your parent, grandparent, or elder is of sound mind, they have a legal right in most countries to make their own healthcare decisions, even if they are diametrically opposed to your own.

At the same time, there are some health situations that would require an adult child to step in—for instance, if you notice early signs of dementia or other rapid changes in their appearance or temperament. Does your elder parent forget things on the stove, or where they live, or just seem suddenly disoriented? This could be a sign of mini strokes, or of a concussion, severe dehydration, low levels of vitamins or minerals like magnesium, or even a bad reaction to a new medication.

You may have to step in and help whether they ask for it or not. Share the details you notice with your parent's doctor or take them for a checkup to see what's at the root of the problem. Try to have your parents choose their healthcare as they do their living situation, but when necessary, intervening quickly could save their lives!

FINANCIAL DECISIONS

Your parents or grandparents may need help with financial decisions, particularly around managing their household or care.

If they choose to and are able to stay at home, how will financial decisions be made? Who will help with household management? If they have to go somewhere with a higher level of care, how does that affect your elders' financial decisions?

As your parents get older, they may start to lose some of their discernment, and unscrupulous, predatory people may try to take advantage of that. One of my elderly neighbors was very philanthropic and very well off. He owned a lot of property and had a lot of money, which he donated to several different charitable organizations.

When his memory and judgment started to falter a bit, somebody came in and convinced him to put all of his money in an account in the Cayman Islands, allegedly to protect it. My neighbor put all his money—millions of dollars—into this account, where it disappeared.

That act threatened the quality of life for this man and his wife in their golden years. He was terribly ashamed, and they had to quickly sell some properties at a loss, just to get back on their feet. He was fortunate to have that option to fall back on, but it also limited what he was able to do for other people because now he had to worry about taking care of himself and his wife.

I've heard all kinds of stories about the sneaky things people will try to do when they think they can take advantage of someone's weakness. As an adult child or caretaker for an older relative, particularly if they're living independently, you will have to keep an eye on what's going on. They may not want to admit falling for a scam. Pay attention to anything that doesn't feel right.

There will still be an adjustment to the change in roles. It may be difficult or embarrassing for your parent to have to admit they can't manage their household by themselves anymore, that they need help.

If your parent is getting more confused or forgetful, you may need to find somebody you trust who can check on them more frequently, if you can't. You may also need to help keep track of their finances, so you can quickly see if anything unexpected appears. You might want to discuss their insurance options, so the cost of their care is manageable and they have the best care possible.

At the end of the day, all of these decisions are in support of giving your parents the best lives possible for their golden years.

TAKE CARE OF THE CARETAKER (THAT'S YOU!)

Your parents need support—but you need support during this time, too.

When I was taking care of everybody, in between hospital runs, I did a lot of thinking and journaling, trying to keep my head on right. I had to hold myself together because it was my time to support them. It felt similar to having a child going through an illness, where you have to show up and be strong because you want them to be strong. You don't want them to feel sorry for themselves. You want to put them in a positive mental space so that they get the best results and outcomes from whatever procedures or situations they have to go through.

But that means you also have to step into a very positive mental place. That's easier said than done, though. These are your parents and you love them and want them to be immortal. You think, "How can this be possible? Why is this happening to me? This only happens to other people!"

Anybody who has gone through this life shift has felt the same way—and we're all going to go there at some point.

During this time, it's important to do whatever you can—meditation, affirmations, journaling—so you can show up as that solid, strong adult for your parents. Your energy is going to determine how your relationship continues, and it can help your bonds grow even stronger.

It gave me strength to think that I was going to honor their choices as best I could because someday, I'm going to go through a similar situation and, when I do, that's what I would want. When I had a hard time making a decision, I would ask myself, "How would I feel in this situation?"

We tend to share some characteristics with our relatives, so reframing the situation in this way can help you put yourself in their shoes. Sometimes, as you're considering what your relative would want, the answer is, "They love me so much that they would say, 'Please go take a break. Go have dinner with your family. Go take care of yourself.'"

As much as you feel like you've got to be there every second, would you as a parent want that for your child? No, you'd want them to go to the gym or have dinner and be with their children, or get their nails done.

Your parents want that for you. They want you to have positive self-care. They want you to not be exhausted or guilty about not being there around the clock. It's common sense, but in the middle of the situation, we don't think about that. Know that they want what's best for you too, and honor that. They may not be able to take care of you anymore, but they still want you to take care of yourself.

And sometimes you just have to let somebody else be the bad guy, the doctor or nurse or whoever else is there. Then you get to slip back into the role of the loving child who is there to support them.

OTHER PEOPLE DON'T GET IT UNLESS THEY'VE BEEN THERE

One way to take care of yourself is to try to maintain your supportive relationships—but sometimes people just don't understand what you're going through.

During this rock-bottom situation in my life, I wanted to spend time with my friends, yet I had to prioritize caring for my elders. My friends didn't have all these relatives to care for and most didn't have six children either! They would say, "Why don't you just relax or come out and have fun with us?"

The reality was, I had so much responsibility being the main parent, breadwinner, and decision-maker for my elders that it was all I could do to keep things going. After a while, my friends just stopped calling.

The gift was that I also had friends in my community who were twice my age and who had parents and grandparents going through similar experiences. These women were my mentors and had a solid footing in this game of changing roles from child to adult to caregiver.

During the time period when I was caring for all of my relatives and working, I ran late for an obstetrician appointment. I called and they told me to still come in, but when I met with the doctor, she was upset. I apologized and explained that I had an emergency call with a doctor, but she didn't understand—because she had never had to care for a relative.

Later, her mother went through a serious illness and passed away, and my obstetrician had to take time off. That's when it really hit her. She apologized for getting upset that day: "You were telling me about your situation, but I just couldn't even fathom it. I'm so sorry."

You'll have friends and other people who aren't in that same boat of responsibility—who aren't caring for elder parents—who won't understand that you may not be as social as you previously were. Or you might have to change plans to go take care of something that comes up suddenly.

With those people, you are just going to have to set that boundary. You don't have to give too much information, and you can do it in a loving way, but it's very necessary to stand up for yourself and what you need to do.

Ultimately, you'll discover that some people are fair-weather friends. Those are the people who don't want to deal with what you're going through; they're just offended that you couldn't make it to their Tupperware party. You'll most likely lose some of these friends, but what you'll find is your tried-and-true, *real* friends.

Some of those true friends still may not be equipped to talk about your experience in depth or advise you about it, so you'll want to have a strong circle of women of different ages and experiences. If you don't already have that in your life, you can join the community of women going through life reboots at www.SheilaMac.com/elders. That will also allow you to find and share different resources for whatever your particular need is at the moment, whether that's how to deal with someone with diabetes, dementia, or Alzheimer's.

Your real friends will also be able to give you love and support. They can help you take your mind off of what you're going through. You can connect and go dancing or swimming or out to dinner and just enjoy being with some of the people who know you the best and love you no matter what.

APPLYING THE BOOTS FORMULA TO ELDERCARE
BEING

For years, I had to show up and be strong for my relatives. When my dad was going through another surgery for cancer, I showed up with a smile so that he felt as happy as possible, instead of being sad that I was sad. It's not that I never showed emotion—as you learned in the Grief chapter, I cried in my quiet hours—but I had to be strong for a loved one going through something.

So who are you going to be when you show up for your parents? A child, someone your parent still feels responsible for and has to take care of, or an adult who can help them make decisions on the level of a partner?

ORIENTATION

The situation is what it is. Your mom had a stroke, or your dad has cancer. Everything is different, and you have to go through this. It's not better than it is, it's not worse than it is, but this is it now. What are you going to do?

You're not responsible for what's happening to your parents, but you may be responsible for what happens next.

It can be a shock to find out that somebody you've always looked up to in your life, the person who took care of you, now needs you to be the guide. It's a humbling experience, and it's a powerful way to honor your parents, but it means that no matter how old you are, you have to grow up even more to take on these responsibilities.

It's hard to assume that role and let go of the fact that you can no longer lean on them; now, they're leaning on you. So now you have to find your strength.

For me, I thought that if I was in their shoes, I'd hope that I would have somebody who cared enough and was strong enough to help me out. I know who I am, and I know my integrity, so I chose to show up and give back out of my heart.

Part of your Orientation is to decide where you're at and how much you're going to participate. Look honestly and truthfully at how much you can do—without going downhill yourself—so you can give the best results, both for taking care of your parents and your own needs. If you're lucky enough to have siblings or other family members working together on this, you can split up the time and extra costs. Sharing the responsibility also allows you to strategize effectively so that you're all contributing to getting the best care for your loved one.

ORDER OF OPERATIONS

The first Order of Operations is also part of Orientation: you have meetings with doctors and advisors and advocates for their health and finances on your side so you can understand the situation as much as possible. And then you make a good action plan, involving your parents as much as possible, so they still have ownership of their lives.

THINKING

What is your mindset? What is the vision? What is the best quality of life this person you're caring for can have? You also have to get your elder to see that vision of the best quality of life given the situation at hand. If they can't tell you, you know them—what do you think they would want?

And what's possible for you while you're dealing with this extra responsibility on top of everything else you do?

I still had to run my business and take care of my children, but some other things had to go. Maybe the house wasn't perfect. I had to adjust my standards a little. I didn't get to the gym as much, though I did prioritize self-care. I just had to remind myself that this is a season.

STEPPING UP

Step up to do what needs to be done, but you also have to step up and honor what they would want you to do. Step up with logic, love, and compassion.

FROM ELDERCARE ROCK BOTTOM TO MOMENT OF EMPOWERMENT

My relatives and I had to figure out each person's situations, one step at a time, with a lot of concessions made and many hours of talking and working with the doctors.

When I was younger, there were a lot of hard times where that parent-child relationship wasn't always there. But when they got sick, I was able to carve out the time to spend with them and we had some beautiful, open conversations. Past hurts were healed. It was empowering to have an adult relationship with my parents on a whole new level of respect and love. They were still my parents, but they also became my best friends.

To be able to reclaim those relationships and take it a step farther was very powerful and healing for all of us going through this difficult time.

When taking care of all these people, I knew there was an end in sight—but that wasn't a positive thing. So my moment of empowerment was being able to give this great care to my family, to give back to the people who had given to me. And now, after going through that in my own life, I can relate to people who are currently going through it. The gift is being able to help guide them to find compassion for their family members—and themselves.

Re-BOOT Activity: Staying Social

Your parent may need you to step in, especially after their own grieving or other rock-bottom situation. Many times, with a health issue or loss of a spouse or close friends, a parent may start to isolate. When a senior begins to emotionally or socially isolate, their brain sits unchallenged. This isolation is a huge risk factor for depression, as well as loss of physical fitness, and could lead to serious health problems.

Being surrounded by friends and loved ones, however, keeps an aging adult's mind active and sharp. Staying involved in the community will help a maturing parent feel more motivated, remain active, take care of their personal appearance, and engage in intellectually stimulating activities.

Here are some ideas for helping your parent to stay social:

☐ Check in with family and friends who are willing to attend activities with your parent. Or, better yet, invite your parent to social activities with others in their peer group if possible.

☐ Look into local clubs and classes that your parent may be interested in. Places to look include the local community, recreational activities, or senior center. Meetup.com, YMCAs, and health clubs also offer options that may be fun!

☐ Your parent may be interested in volunteering at an animal shelter, school, or political campaigns.

☐ Transportation issues: If your parent is no longer safe to drive, check into community programs like Access or Dial-A-Ride. There is always Uber and Lyft, which have made getting around in major cities worldwide hassle-free and far more affordable than in the past. (Your parent may need help with the app, or you can book a ride from your smartphone!)

If you feel concerned that your adult parent may need further help or is not functioning safely at home alone, contact their doctor to see if assisted-living situations would be an option. It is always important to seek medical advice immediately if there is a significant and sudden change in your parent's personality, memory, or ability to function, as it may be signs of something far more serious than a failing memory or aging. The faster you get them medical attention, the better the chances your parent will have a full or better recovery. A very accurate treatment or living arrangement plan helps your parent have the best quality of life possible.

🎁 *My Gift to You* 🎁

Dear Readers,

Once I realized how sacred and fleeting time was with my beloved elders, that's when I started to create ways to care for my elders while living a balanced lifestyle. If you desire to give the elder parent or loved one in your life the best of care and quality time, while also caring for your career, family and not neglecting yourself; then this gift is for you.

Go to www.SheilaMac.com/elderreboot to receive the e-book: *A Re-BOOT for Eldercare "How to Give the Gift of Time to Yourself and Your Loved One When It Matters Most."*

CHAPTER 9

BREAKING THE CYCLE (ADDICTION)

Maggie grew up loved by her relatives and friends.

Shortly after coming into this world, she was adopted. Her birth mother had addiction problems and got pregnant very young. Close relatives arranged Maggie's adoption by two loving parents who couldn't have children of their own.

Maggie grew up in a beautiful environment. She was well cared for, went to the top schools, and had private tutoring when she needed it. She loved horseback riding, ice skating, and hours and hours spent with her parents. They loved Maggie and gave her everything they possibly could.

Then, toward the end of high school, Maggie's dad got sick and died. Maggie had received a full scholarship to college, but she deferred admission for a year, so she could stay home and help her mom through the grieving process. She didn't feel like she could leave until her mom was settled and in a healthy place.

Financially, they had to adjust. They sold the house Maggie had grown up in and moved to a smaller one across town. She finished high school, but one by one her friends left for college and Maggie stayed at home.

In high school, Maggie hung out with friends and had a beer or smoked a little pot—or whatever kids do that we don't want them to do. As her friends went away to college and she grieved her father's death in her own way—she began hanging with a new crowd and experimenting with harder drugs.

Maggie's mother was going through her grieving process, so she wasn't quite as present as she'd been in the past. She missed the signs that Maggie was slipping into addiction. If she had thought about it, she probably would have believed she knew and trusted her daughter. Experimenting with hard drugs wasn't a behavior she would suspect from the child she knew.

While Maggie hung out with her friends, Maggie's mom went to grief counseling. By the time she noticed the changes in Maggie's behavior, the situation was severe. Maggie wasn't working, she wasn't doing anything. She stole money from her mom and friends. When her old high school friends came back to visit from college, they wondered what happened and who this new person was. It was very painful for those friends to see this young woman they loved so much go down such a difficult, terrible road. She lost a lot of friends who didn't want to hang out with somebody doing that to themselves.

Maggie didn't get to go to college the next year. She lost her scholarship. Now her mom had to go through a new grieving process: losing the version of the little girl she thought she knew.

FILLING A VOID

People aren't born smokers or alcoholics, but they may be at risk for addiction. Maggie's birth mother was an addict; it's possible that Maggie inherited an increased likelihood of addictive behavior. Beyond that risk, however, Maggie was also trying to fill a void. Many times, people try to kill the pain of grief or loss with drugs, alcohol, cigarettes, or eating disorders.

People who exhibit addictive behaviors are filling something in their life that they don't feel empowered about, that they feel they don't have control over. So, they go down that road as an escape route. They can't deal with it, so they go drink or smoke pot. Sometimes it's only a couple of drinks or smoking a little for a brief period of time. Other times it's a slippery slope to higher level, hardcore drugs that can lead to an overdose. Whether it's lighter substances, even cigarettes, or hardcore drugs, when the substance controls you instead of you controlling your use, that's a sign of addiction.

The things people are addicted to vary from one person to the next, whether it's a drug, a food, alcohol, or an activity that's bad for you. People have sexual addictions, addictions to gambling or shopping. Unbalanced behavior without moderation is another sign of addiction. Whatever form it takes, addiction can lead straight to rock bottom.

I don't believe addicts choose to be addicts. They want to escape or numb a painful situation and use the substance or activity to do so. What begins as perhaps an entertaining, one-off experiment, triggers the feel-better part of their brain and when things are bad again, they go do the behavior again to feel better and it becomes a vicious, uncontrollable cycle. When a chemical is involved, it's not easy to control. If it were, addicts would be able to say, "Well, I'm done. I'm not going to do that anymore."

If you can't control the behavior, it's an addiction. Whether you see that in yourself or in a loved one, you need support and a community, so you don't have to go through that alone. It's going to take a lot of willpower and other resources to get through. You may want to help the loved one who has an addiction with all your heart, but you're going to have to do more than just talk about it.

WHAT TO DO IF YOU RECOGNIZE ADDICTION IN YOURSELF

If you're reading this book and going through an addiction yourself, struggling to pull away and wanting to live the life you envisioned but your addiction continues to pull you back down, know that, for your children, for yourself, for the life that you desire: you're going to have to put down that addiction. If you don't, we have an activity at the end of this chapter that shows how your addiction affects every single aspect of your life. If your addiction is controlling you and you're not in control of your life, you need to consider seeking medical treatment for an addiction.

If you recognize addictive behavior in yourself, maybe this just solidifies it, or maybe it brings it to light for you. You thought things were going fine and then you realize, "Oh, that's why my family isn't speaking to me," or, "That's why I'm having such a tough time at work and always getting in trouble."

I recently met a thirty-two-year-old waiter who works two jobs but is still struggling to pay his rent because he goes out drinking most nights of the week. All of his friends drink, his family drinks, and that's the only way he knows how to socialize. Anything he does outside of work involves alcohol, and it's starting to mess up his life. He's tired all the time, he doesn't feel well most days, and he wants to find one well-paying job instead of working two lower-paying ones. As we talked, he finally admitted, "I think I have a problem with my drinking."

If you've had a similar realization, you may be wondering what you should do—or what you *can* do.

You have to address the real cause of what led you down that road, honor your experience, and face it, then deal with whatever you have to do to get rid of some of it. That may require medical intervention, medication to get off the drug, or going through a rehab program because now your body is physically addicted to the substance.

You may need to find a new peer group who are focused on the positive things you want to accomplish, like work, school, or personal development. You need to change your environment so that you set yourself up for success, removing the people, situations, or items that trigger your addiction.

Then, you need to replace your addiction with a new, healthy behavior. What can you replace this coping mechanism with?

Some people get a high when they run, and that allows them to process the things that are happening in their life. Or if running isn't where you're at right now, maybe you want to try yoga to help you get calm and centered. There has to be something new that you pick up instead of picking up that drug or alcohol or credit card or food to binge on.

If you used to be addicted to burgers and fries, maybe you can get addicted to going out dancing or doing yoga or riding your bike. You can replace an addiction to drinking or a drug with writing in your journal, blasting music, or painting when things are difficult. Maybe you're going to go join an adult sports team. We don't have to stop playing just because we're adults.

I have a client who used to be a competitive swimmer. That was her healthy release and way to cope.

Then she had children and got stuck working long hours in a job she didn't like. She was doing everything for everyone else and nothing for herself. So, to cheer herself, she would eat little treats. One day, when her kids were in high school, she realized just how out of shape she was. Thinking back, she also realizes that she's been miserable for years. She's not happy, so she numbed her misery with food.

She struggled with that realization. She was angry. She asked herself, "What the hell happened to me?"

After dealing with her immediate reaction, she decided to take a plunge and make one change for herself. One of the neighbors let her use their pool in exchange for teaching their children how to swim. Soon, she started teaching other children how to swim as well. Eventually, she started her own swimming school.

Now, she's in great shape, and she still teaches swimming. Her kids are grown, and she taught her grandkids how to swim— and she's happy. She needed a way to replace that addiction with something positive.

Your healthy replacement doesn't have to be expensive. It doesn't have to please another human being. It's just something that is your way of expressing yourself or having fun that isn't eating or doing something else to fill the void. Then it's a real happiness, not a drug-induced feeling from an activity that drags you down. It's a healthy habit.

That leads to taking back that control of your life, rather than letting your addiction determine where you end up.

WHAT TO DO IF YOU RECOGNIZE ADDICTION IN A LOVED ONE

As I said, addiction affects everyone and everything in your life. But what does it look like for the person on the other side of that addiction?

You may experience a child, friend, or partner struggle with an addiction. But you can't just tell them, "Oh, just stop drinking. Get addicted to the beach!" That's a great idea, but when it's not your own idea, it won't work. And then you'll have the added resentment of, "Who the hell are you to tell me what to do?"

Sometimes people say things they wouldn't say if they weren't in that addiction space. Their character and personality are almost lost; it's not them. They have something else that's ruling their common sense or right thinking. If they were in control, in their right mind, and not addicted to something, they would not want the addiction in their life, your life, or their children's lives.

When somebody's ready to kick an addiction, they ask, "What can I do? What are my options?"

They're ready to walk through that door instead of you having to push them. I know that you want to push them, because you love them so much. You have the desire to push them, drag them, do whatever you have to do—figuratively or literally—just to get them to that healthy place because you want the best for them.

Sometimes that means stepping out of the picture, using tough love, or setting boundaries.

You have to be set, solid, unwavering on your boundaries. You might have to say, "I can't have this in the house. If you come home drunk, then you're going to have to go until you get treatment." If you say you're going to do something, you need to follow through with it. Then you make that person go somewhere else—a friend's house, a hotel—so they know their behavior is not acceptable. When that person isn't drunk, they wouldn't want that for you or your children, so this is the boundary. This has happened; third strike, and you're out.

You can't control the other person's outcome. You can't make the decision for them. You can't push any more. But you can decide, say, for this six months or a year—or even for a day—that you are not going to let it ruin how you show up for work or for yourself or with your kids.

They will feel the difference. The strongest people I've known have had to do that. And their loved ones are most often the ones who actually get help and treatment because they're following through. They understand this is the way it's got to be and that you're not playing games. You're not joining that club; you're modeling the strength that somebody in an addiction doesn't have at the moment.

YOU BOTH NEED SUPPORT

Someone suffering from an addiction needs a lot of help once they are ready to seek treatment—but their loved ones need support as well.

You need resources, a peer group, and support from other people and the community to help somebody get through their addiction. You don't just need one support group; you're going to need a lot of support groups. You're going to need every single thing you can get, any person or group you can have on your side. You need as many people as possible to help get somebody back on that beautiful track to a good life. I've included some resources for support on my website; that link is at the end of this chapter.

Having a group and some support lets you know that you're not alone. You didn't cause this. It can happen to anyone from any group. Addiction does not discriminate. You can give someone the best possible life on this planet, and they could still have an addiction.

You can give and receive help, but whether or not the other person takes it is out of your control. Sometimes the only thing you can do is send somebody love. If they're hurting you or stealing from you because of this addiction, the only way to be safe may be to keep them at arm's length and let another group or resource step in and help you through that.

That's okay, because that is probably the safest and healthiest thing for both of you. It's tough love. It's sending compassionate, loving energy. It's living your life and doing your routine and setting those boundaries, so you're not dragged into it. It's getting your own help, through different connections and groups that are designed for people that have people with addictions in their life. That connection to other people helps a lot.

Somebody in an addiction needs to hear it from different people. They need to look in the mirror—but they need people to guide them to that mirror. The people closest to them are usually not the people who are actually going to get through to them. They need a different voice or perspective.

At the same time, it's easy to have a loved one pull you into that drama. If you get caught in their trauma drama, it's like trying to rescue someone who is drowning—more often than not, they're going to pull you down with them. You love them, but you are at risk of losing your own life and losing yourself.

CODEPENDENCE

If you're mentally getting dragged down, you're already drowning with them.

It's very easy to go down the codependent tunnel or give support in a way that actually adds to the other person's addiction. Codependence can happen when someone ends up covering for the addiction. They cover it up, compensate, don't take care of themselves, don't do their own self-care. Their whole life is run by the other person—but it's really the addiction that's running both of their lives.

When you enable somebody in their addiction, it just prolongs the pain. You can become addicted to trying to help this person and you lose your other healthy relationships. You lose your life. You're spending so much money and time enabling the addict that you're not taking care of yourself—that can easily happen.

People get so caught up in thinking they have to help this person, that they have to do whatever they can, they forget to help themselves. Give yourself permission to say, "This is what I need to do to let that relationship be healthy again." Accept that it may not happen right away. It may not happen at all.

But don't take on the burden of a responsibility that isn't yours.

Live your life and model what a healthy life looks like. Don't let this situation disrupt all the good that you're doing. You're the healthy, grounded one who can guide them out—even when guiding them out means stepping away and giving tough love. You need to be really centered and have control of your life, so you don't go down with them.

In the activities section of this chapter, there are some questions to determine whether you may be enabling a loved one's addiction. You will also find suggestions on how to stay the course of supporting your loved one through an addiction without losing your own wellness in the process. You and the other family members not dealing with addiction are the healthier ones in this case, so setting solid boundaries will model wellness to your loved one. It is important to have all parents and other family members involved and aligned on how to set and enforce loving boundaries that will protect everyone's safety and help the loved one recover. Show them their options and discuss the resources for support. Show them their light and focus on their strengths.

ADDICTIONS FEED ON ATTENTION

When you feed an addiction by giving it attention, you fuel it on an energetic realm. As Tony Robbins says, "Energy goes where attention flows."

It's important to not fuel that fire.

Put your energy on the things that you can control and change in your life. What can you do as a parent or partner in a relationship? What are the things you can control? Because you can't control another human being.

You can control how you give attention when the person with the addiction has a success, when they're really making the effort, when they are going to get help or going to a treatment center—that's when you give the attention. You can focus on that and on their strengths and remind them of who they really are, who they showed up as in your life. You're supporting every little teeny-tiny good effort.

The message is: "I love you. Because I love you, I'm not going to support you when you're doing this. And because I also love and honor myself, I know you wouldn't want that for me—and I don't want that for you. I don't want to see you hurt yourself. I'm not going to help you hurt yourself. I will support your efforts to love yourself."

If you're not the one with the addiction, you have the choice of how to show up. You're teaching people how to show up for you by how you show up for them and for yourself.

WHAT IF THE ADDICTION ISN'T TO DRUGS OR ALCOHOL?

We've focused a lot on addictions to drugs or alcohol, but what if it's something different? What if it's an addiction to gambling, to cigarettes, or an eating disorder?

The concept is going to be the same, but the treatment is different.

There are certain levels of a relationship where you might step in. Maybe you can keep your loved one active and give them fun things to do that take them out of the place they use addiction to escape. You're doing something to get them out of that mental state or place of feeling down that brings them to that addiction sometimes.

What can you change in the addictive pattern? You're not saying, "Hey let's stop shopping." Instead, it might be, "Hey, let's take a road trip. Let's go to the gym. Let's go dancing." Then you're taking them away from it and replacing it with something as a couple, as a parent, or as a friend. You're redirecting the focus without having the discussion about shopping. Then they're having fun and they didn't have to face that issue for a while.

Compliment them on things that are real. Not a fake compliment, but a real, heartfelt compliment on the positive things. Positive reinforcement helps them keep wanting to do whatever earned that compliment.

Nobody wants to be criticized. Constructive criticism, especially when someone's in a place of going into an addiction as a coping mechanism for everything else that's going on in their life, is not really helpful. They don't need you to throw a rock at them right now. They're already hurting. You see that they're hurting. Give them a hand and help them up. Get them out of that mental state, go do something else. Let them see that it's coming from love, so they feel only love.

If you have a relationship that allows for an open conversation about the addiction, you can say, "Hey, if you start going down that road again, what can I do to help you?" Maybe you can come up with a code word, or they can tell you something to do or not do. Then you know how to support them through the rough spots without being overbearing.

Then you can say, "Remember that we had that talk? I see you're going down there, and you said to do these things, so I'm doing them. If you want me to stop, I will, but I'm going to support you this way."

That takes a lot of the judgment out of it. You don't think you're better than them because you don't have that addiction, and you're not telling them not to do it because you know better. It's just, "I'm here and I'm going to support you as best I can."

That helps you and your loved one reach the desired outcome a lot faster.

APPLYING THE BOOTS FORMULA TO ADDICTION

I once worked with a very successful businessman named Ben, a friend of a friend, who hid his extreme alcoholism for years. Eventually, however, it caught up with him. He got into a car accident, totaled his car, got charged with a DUI, and lost his license. After that, he didn't hide his drinking as much and, during a days-long binge, he fell into a pool and almost drowned. His friend came to me afraid that Ben was going to die. Ben's addiction was threatening his life.

BEING

Ben first had to acknowledge who he was Being: an alcoholic.

He needed a reboot instead of another rehab, because he wanted to redefine his identity and become functional again. If he didn't want to change, nobody could make him. He had to be willing to take these steps.

So who are you Being if you are the one with an addiction? Or who are you going to be when you're showing up for this person suffering from an addiction? You first have to admit that there's a problem before you can begin walking through it.

When you start to show up again, the people around you see a different person showing up—and they see the effort. It brings that positive healing to everybody around you. And as you inspire them, they can reinspire you as you see people in your life choosing to make a change or pick up healthier habits. That's a healthy cycle that reinforces the change you made.

ORIENTATION

Ben had to acknowledge that his addiction owned him. He had to confront how many times he put himself or others in danger. He had to look at how much money his drinking had cost—and what the cost was in health, quality of life, safety, and how other people perceived him. Ben had to own up to that before he could switch roles.

He also had to acknowledge the good parts of himself: his intelligence and good business sense (when he was sober) and all the people his company helped. Then he had to say, "This is what I would like for my business, my family, and myself."

Where are you in your life, and how can you take ownership of your situation?

When you make a mistake or something doesn't go right or you get a surprise, you can be honest about that too. People really appreciate that and can support you through falling off that horse or wagon, which will happen. In life, there are going to be challenges, and how you show up through them is huge. People are going to support you when you're willing to be open and honest. When you don't hide anything, it's easier to get the help you need quickly to get back on track easily.

ORDER OF OPERATIONS

Once Ben knew what his life currently looked like and how he wanted it to change, he figured out the steps to get from point A to point B.

The first step was to clean up his environment. He invited his friends and family to his dumping party, and we dumped many dollars' worth of very expensive booze down the drain. He was honest with people about where he wanted to go, and he asked them for their support. They agreed not to cover for him, to help him set boundaries, and to model healthy behavior.

What are the steps you need to take to replace your addiction with a healthier alternative? What are the steps you need to put in place to set boundaries and model healthy behavior for a friend or loved one with an addiction?

THINKING

Ben had to change his Thinking, too. He had to be honest and think differently about his life while giving himself credit for his successes.

When he had a setback, he asked, "How do I change that? What do I need to do differently next time? Who do I need to talk to, to get support on this?"

So how can you change your mindset? How can you think differently about yourself and what you want your life to look like? If you can see the end of the addiction, then you can live into it.

STEPPING UP

Ben stepped up into a big change, and that was the moment he saved his own life.

We all have challenges every day. When you step up and face these challenges, you show yourself and everyone around you that *you* are in control of your life. So step into taking care of yourself, loving yourself, and empowering yourself to be the best *you* can be.

FROM ADDICTION ROCK BOTTOM TO MOMENT OF EMPOWERMENT

Maggie hit a literal rock bottom. People were concerned she would end up homeless and lost, unsure if she would live or die.

Her friends and family did an intervention and got her into rehab, which cost a lot of money but got her back on her feet. It took a couple of years and a few backslides. She would get better and then fall off the wagon and have to go through the whole process again—but each successive time, she didn't fall as deep and it didn't last as long.

Maggie finally went to university, graduated, and got a good job. She never returned to that low point in her life.

Re-BOOT Activity: Free Yourself from Addictions

We all either face or know someone who has faced addiction.

The following is some additional information that may help you or loved ones take back your power and rebuild your life.

- Excessive alcohol use can increase a person's risk of developing serious health problems in addition to those issues associated with intoxication behaviors and alcohol withdrawal symptoms.
- Tobacco use and smoking do damage to nearly every organ in the human body, often leading to lung cancer, respiratory disorders, heart disease, stroke, and other illnesses.
- Marijuana has not only immediate effects like distorted perception, difficulty problem solving, and loss of motor coordination but also effects with long-term use such as respiratory infection, impaired memory, and exposure to cancer-causing compounds.
- Opioids, including prescription drugs such as hydrocodone, oxycodone, morphine, and codeine, reduce the perception of pain but can also produce drowsiness, mental confusion, euphoria, nausea, constipation, and—depending upon the amount of drug taken—can depress breathing.
- Opioid misuse represents a unique challenge. According to the Center for Disease Control and Prevention, an average of 130 Americans die every day from an opioid overdose.
- As people use opioids repeatedly, their tolerance increases, and they may not be able to maintain the source for the drugs. This can cause them to turn to illegal sources for these drugs and even switch from prescription drugs to cheaper and more risky substitutes like heroin. These substances vary in purity and strength, which increases the risk of serious medical complications or overdose. It's not worth the risk, ever. There

are many medically supervised programs to help a person to reduce and then get off these drugs completely.

- While many can benefit from using these medications to manage pain, prescription drugs are frequently misused. If you ever have to take prescription medications for pain, make sure you take the lowest dose possible.
- Alternative pain management options can be used along with regular medication. Some people have had great success using Arnica cream and homeopathic pills to reduce pain and swelling. This always must be discussed with your doctor first to ensure it will not have a side effect with any prescriptions or other treatment methods you are using.
- Acupuncture, chiropractic, earthling mats for sleeping, and physical therapy may be great additions to a healing program and are a good way to help with pain management control.

Quiz to see if you or a loved one may have a drug or alcohol addiction:

☐ You or your loved one uses references to alcohol or drugs in many conversations, like, "I can see us sitting by the pool relaxing and having a drink or smoking some pot."

☐ You or a loved one keeps taking a drug after it's no longer needed for a health problem.

☐ You or your loved one often will even look in other people's medicine cabinets for drugs to take.

☐ You or your loved one has all but lost interest in things that once brought a good amount of happiness to life.

☐ You or your loved one needs more and more of a substance to get the same effects.

☐ You or your loved one hides the drug use from others. Getting caught causes an outburst.

☐ You or your loved one takes prescribed meds with alcohol or other drugs.

☐ You or your loved one often feels strange when the drug wears off. You may be shaky, depressed, sick to your stomach, sweat, or have migraines.

☐ You or your loved one goes to more than one doctor to get prescriptions to treat the same drug addiction.

☐ You or your loved one has a new set of friends with whom doing drugs is the routine.

☐ You or your loved one just can't stop using the drug, even if you want to. You are still using it even though it's making bad things happen in life, like trouble with friends, family, work, or the law.

☐ Other people start to complain to you about how you or your loved one has changed and not for the positive. You sleep too much or too little, compared with how you used to. Or you eat a lot more or less than before.

☐ You or your loved one spends a lot of time thinking about the drug: how to get more, when you'll take it, how good you feel, or how bad you feel afterward.

☐ You or your loved one is having trouble getting along with coworkers, teachers, friends, or family members.

☐ You or your loved one has lost track of boundaries and limits in relationships as well as in how much of a drug to ingest. It is never enough and it's often way too much.

☐ You or your loved one drives or does other dangerous actives while intoxicated.

☐ You or a loved one borrows or steals money to pay for drugs.

☐ You or your loved one looks different. Things to watch for are bloodshot eyes, bad breath, shakes/tremors, frequent bloody noses, or rapid weight gain or weight loss.

☐ You or your loved one has trouble doing normal daily things, like cooking or working, and often either oversleeps or has severe insomnia.

When giving an addiction the boot, get everyone in the family on board:

- Get professional help for yourself and your loved one.
- Get community support for yourself and your loved one.
- Prepare yourself for the fact that there will be ups, downs, and sideways situations before recovery is completed.
- Be patient with yourself and your loved ones.
- Take care of yourself and the other people in your family.
- Believe your loved one's actions rather than their words.

At first when a family or group of friends come together to help a loved one give addiction the boot, the loved one may show anger or be in denial. With patience and as much support as you can gather, your loved one will one day thank you for sticking with them through this time.

Bonus Re-BOOT: Are You Enabling an Addiction?

Are you enabling your spouse, family member, friend, or loved one?

Enabling contributes to the problem. Enabling a loved one to continue an unhealthy and dangerous habit such as drug or alcohol abuse is a huge contribution to your loved one staying stuck in an abusive pattern.

If you suspect that a loved one has an addiction problem, take the quiz below. If you notice you and your loved one's extended family and friends are following these enabling patterns, it is time to work together to make a change.

☐ Have you ever called in sick to school or work for your loved one even though you knew they could have made it?
☐ Have you set consequences for your loved one's problem behaviors but failed to follow through on them?
☐ Do you blame yourself for things that your loved one trapped in addiction is doing?
☐ Do you let your addictive loved one get away with just about anything, no matter what you do?
☐ Do you or others in your household say things like, "It's our fault for not being here more"?
☐ Have you or your family and friends paid legal fees or other charges as a result of your loved one's actions while under the influence?
☐ Do you or your family and friends ever lie to the others in your community to cover up your loved one's drunk or drugged behavior?

For further resources for help on an addiction or life reboot, I have a resource section in this book, and the most current updates can be found on my website. My goal is to make sure that as you heal on your terms, you can connect to as many resources as possible. It is imperative that you take massive action when dealing with the throes of an addiction; the more resources a person or family has, the higher the chance of a full recovery.

🎁 *My Gift to You* 🎁

Dear Readers,

Protect yourself and your loved one from the controlling manipulative difficulties of abuse. Learn how to defend against backsliding and help to re-BOOT your addiction from one that controls you or a loved one to a healthy habit that blesses all.

Get your two-week, e-mail-based *Addiction Defense Course* at: www.SheilaMac.com/defense.

CHAPTER 10

SELF-CARE AND SPIRITUALITY

Lisa's husband passed away. As a couple, they had recently agreed that they were going to sell their house and move to a retirement community—and now she had to do that alone. Between the loss of her husband and the home her son had grown up in, Lisa was hit with a double whammy of grief.

As anyone who has lost someone knows, grief causes stress levels to rise exponentially. On top of that, selling a house and moving—even when it's a planned, happier move—is also stressful and can be unsettling. You lose things, objects get broken, and you have to readjust to a new place.

Lisa wasn't just moving away from the house where she'd raised her son, she was also leaving the neighborhood she'd lived in for forty-five years, where her friends lived, and where she volunteered in the community. She felt she was losing everything in her life at once.

Lisa and I started talking because she needed some support through all these decisions and upheaval. She was even overwhelmed with things she was usually quite good at—her paperwork and taxes—because of all the changes she was going through at once.

As we talked, she told me how she took care of her husband, her son, and her community. But she had never taken time for herself, and now she was faced with too much time.

I gave her the challenge of doing one thing for herself every day, as if she was doing it for her husband or closest friend. If someone showed up on her doorstep in pain, stressed out, or going through something, Lisa would drop everything to help that person. Now, though, that person would be her—she was going to give herself as much attention, honor, and love as she gave to so many other people—and I asked her to send me pictures of her doing these things, so she would be held accountable.

At first, she was like, "Are you crazy?"

I promised her it would help—even though she thought it would be dumb. "For me," I told her. "Do it for me if you're not going to do it for yourself."

The first day, Lisa sent me a picture of herself getting her nails done with the text, "I haven't had my nails done in months, not since before Dave got sick. It felt so good, and you were right—I kind of needed that break."

"Great!" I replied. "What are you doing tomorrow?"

FROM SURVIVAL MODE TO SELF-CARE

When we hit rock-bottom situations in life, it tends to send us into survival mode. And when we're in that place, we're so busy making ends meet, struggling with grief, loss, and pain, and dealing what whatever is going on that we don't have a choice but to eliminate some of the things we usually do.

When you have to go to work, then go visit somebody in the hospital, then pick up your kids, and you *still* have to make dinner and maintain a certain level of cleanliness in your home or whatever duties you have to do, taking an hour for yourself, to go to the gym or meditate, gets pushed aside. "It's just today," you tell yourself. But then tomorrow comes and goes, and another day and another. The next thing you know, it's been a month or two, and then you really start to notice the difference. One day, you wake up and you're not who you used to be.

When you aren't practicing self-care, it shows up all over. Maybe you're exhausted and not sleeping right. Maybe you're off your healthy diet. Perhaps you've pushed your meditation practice, and it's showing up at work or with relationships. You start snapping at people you would never snap at.

When you're already at rock bottom with one situation and then you realize how many of your healthy habits went in the fallout, it can be overwhelming. You've hit another rock bottom, and you may be looking around and thinking, "How do I get from here back to where I was?"

You start over.

ONE STEP AT A TIME

Starting over sounds scary, but there is good news. Your muscles have memory. Your body remembers healthy eating. And you can catch up on your sleep.

But it's not going to happen in one day.

It took you more than one day to reach this rock-bottom place. One day of not cleaning up doesn't bring a mess into your life. One day of extra spending doesn't necessarily lead to a negative cash flow situation. So it's going to take a few days—or even weeks—to get back to where you were.

The fastest way to start climbing up from rock bottom is to take small steps and focus on little wins. Do one small chore that's fallen by the wayside, and then one reward to yourself and do one small act of self-care, too. As you do one, the other becomes easier and you climb back up from your rock bottom.

Once you've taken that first step and have that first little win, you can take another. Maybe tomorrow you'll clean one part of your house or deal with one bill that got thrown into a pile. Set a goal or a timer and once you reach that number or that time, stop and take some time to reward yourself for the progress you've made.

Just for tonight, take five minutes to meditate. It doesn't have to be the whole hour that you used to do, as long as you're doing *something*. Maybe you're starting over with your budget, so you can't go get a massage or facial or have a spa day right now. Just for today, try doing your nails at home. Or just for this afternoon, take a ten-minute walk. Anything that leaving you thinking, "Oh, that feels better," after you do it.

You can even schedule appointments for time to spoil yourself a little, even if you just mark enough time in your calendar for simple things like lighting a candle and meditating, taking a walk or a nap, or watching a movie—something that's just for you. You'll still have to take the right actions and take care of the things you're required to care for in your life, but you can also honor an appointment with yourself as much as you show up for the other people, or situations, or emergencies that threw you into survival mode in the first place.

Your body and your mind need that break. They need a respite in order to continue getting you from that rock-bottom place back into your life. Without it, it's like not putting fuel in your car and expecting to go on a road trip. You know that sooner or later you're just going to run out of gas.

With your brain and body fueled up and ready to go, however, you will be able to come up with new strategies for resolving whatever issues come up.

YOU DEFINE YOUR SELF-CARE

You have to take care of yourself before you help all of the other people that you care for. Let me say that again: You have to take care of yourself *first*.

Self-care looks different for everybody. It may include:

- Meditating
- Praying or another spiritual practice
- Doing yoga
- Walking
- Running
- Lifting weights
- Playing sports
- Playing a musical instrument
- Seeing a movie
- Dancing
- Journaling
- Reading
- Being in nature
- Gardening
- Horseback riding
- Getting your hair or nails done
- Getting a facial or massage
- Painting a picture or creating art
- Sleeping in or taking a nap as a gift to your body
- Just sitting and being happy doing nothing

What do all of these things have in common? They are activities you do for you. And if you're not used to practicing self-care, how do you get started?

Self-care is individual. It's whatever fills *your* soul, not anybody else's. So first, think about what fuels you. You may have to go back in your memory a couple decades to find something you used to love that has fallen away in your life.

When I was a kid, I was on the swim team. That was my meditation. When things were going wrong at home, I would go swim laps for hours. I still like to swim whenever I can. It doesn't feel like working out; swimming energizes me. I just lose myself in the quiet, peaceful rhythm. It's the best medicine in the world for me.

A friend I used to go to the spa with loves being in the wilderness; for her, it is heaven. Her favorite vacation of all time was a hiking trip where she carried everything in a backpack, went to the bathroom in bushes, and swam naked in the lake. She was one with nature—and that was a spiritual experience for her.

That wouldn't do it for me. I liked the spa because it was elegant. We got massages every day and had a chef preparing our meals. They took care of us. Putting on a backpack, walking across the country, and sleeping in the cold woods would be torture for me.

Self-care is different for everyone. Your partner's definition and your child's definition and your definition of passion and relaxation are probably all going to differ. You have to honor those differences and evaluate what that is for *you*.

How are you going to take a break? What is your release? How do you meditate and relax and refuel? What are those things you've done throughout your life that have caused you to lose all sense of time?

When you're in that flow state, so connected with whatever you're doing that nothing else matters, it gives you that break and that sense of peace.

IT DOESN'T HAVE TO TAKE A LOT OF TIME OR MONEY

I don't want to completely oversimplify things, but self-care doesn't need to be complicated. It doesn't need to cost a lot of money. It doesn't even need to take a lot of time.

You can renew yourself and fuel your soul even on a budget.

When you're at your rock bottom, you probably don't have the time or money to take a big trip and fly to another country, just to sit by the pool and sip coconut drinks. You can still recreate the restful aspect of that vacation in your daily life—without spending thousands of dollars and taking two weeks off work.

Now, I'm not saying never to take vacations. You may want to travel the world or visit loved ones or go to your favorite places. I'm simply saying that you don't *have* to do these things in order to refuel.

We'll talk more about Lifestyle Design in the next chapter, but when you design a life that makes you happy and that lifts you up, you don't have to take a vacation from it. Who wants a life you need to escape because it doesn't fuel your soul?

So where can you build little breaks and mini vacations into your everyday life? You can:

- Find a pool in your neighborhood and enjoy sitting by it
- Go for a swim
- Take a class
- Take a nap
- Trade an hour of babysitting with another family, and use that hour for anything you want

The person who comes back from these mini vacations is not a cranky, exhausted, unhappy person. That person is fueled and relaxed. The little things that would normally bug you will now just roll off your back. You may not even notice! Everybody around you benefits from that brief respite as much as you do.

When you practice self-care and take these little breaks, it's a bonus when you get to do something more elaborate.

TAKE CARE OF YOURSELF INSIDE AND OUT

It's also important to take care of your complete self. Part of that means going to your doctor regularly for whole-body checkups.

I have a friend who was doing everything right—eating healthy and working out—but she kept gaining weight. Nothing was working, so she was ready to give up and go for the pie. Then she went to the doctor and found out that she had a thyroid issue. Other people in her family have the same condition, but she didn't think about it until the doctor brought it up. There was a simple treatment, and now she's enjoying the fruits of her healthy lifestyle.

It's important to determine whether you have a condition that requires medical intervention. Maybe you're low on vitamin D, which can show up as depression, fatigue, getting sick often, or even brittle bones. Perhaps you need a prescription instead of a coping mechanism. Maybe you're not getting the right nutrients or are having a hormonal issue. If you're tired all the time, you may be drinking a lot of caffeine to make up for that—some people even turn to Adderall or other drugs—but your doctor could diagnose a biochemical shift in your body and help you make healthier choices.

Ask to have a complete bloodwork analysis that includes checking your hormone levels, your thyroid, as well as your vitamin D and other major vitamin levels. Many times, a small shift in any one of these areas will cause a person to be overtired, anxious, or to get angry easily. Once any health issues are ruled out or corrected, you may be ready for a lifestyle reboot!

A lot of people don't go to the doctor regularly. Or they treat their symptoms instead of getting to the cause of those symptoms. When you're practicing good self-care, however—when you're taking a holistic view of what's going on with yourself and your body—you're not just treating whatever appears; you're giving your body everything it needs. Making sure your physical and mental health are at the best levels possible will help you stay laser-focused on what matters most to you.

PRACTICE GRATITUDE

There's one practice that takes little time and is free: gratitude.

When you're at this starting over from your rock bottom, you don't get days off. Or your days off are full of the extra work of rebuilding your new life, but expressing gratitude helps you see the positive changes that are happening instead of wallowing in the negative situation. Perhaps you can give thanks for not setting an alarm clock and getting extra sleep one day. When you wake up, say, "Thank you. I'm so grateful I gave myself that rest. That was a beautiful gift, and now I can start the day."

Look for things to be grateful for, and don't forget the small things: your bills got paid, you were able to leave work an hour early and go for a walk. You have a roof over your head, you are fortunate enough to have cherished relationships, or even that you got enough healthful food to eat that day. Make a decision every day, even when you're going through a difficult situation, to find three things to be grateful for and focus on those.

A gratitude practice is a gift you give yourself. Focusing on these good things allows you to be happier and healthier. It keeps you calmer, lowers blood pressure, and improves your mindset. When you focus on the positive, more good things will show up (just like when you're looking for the negative in a situation, your mind starts noticing more of it).

Happiness is a choice. Living in gratitude is a choice. You can't change everything all at once, and it takes time to reboot, but you can enjoy those present moments and enjoy the things you can be grateful for *now* instead of waiting to be happy and grateful once everything is in place and perfect.

Gratitude has become a habit for me. As I write this book, I'm moving into a new home. I lost the other home in the fire I told you about, and I had to struggle for a while to get back on my feet and be able to buy a new home. But now I live in the nicest home I've ever lived in. As I walk through each room,

I express my gratitude for everything I have: "I'm grateful for the granite countertops where I can prepare food for my loved ones. I'm grateful for the hardwood floors where I can practice yoga. I'm grateful for the nice people in the community who welcomed me with open arms and the convenient sports center where I can take care of myself."

And I'm grateful that you are here with me, reading this book.

SPIRITUALITY

Part of your gratitude practice might also tie in with any spiritual practices you have.

People have different belief systems and spiritual traditions that often come from how they were raised. Those beliefs and traditions can be very healing, centering, and grounding—especially for someone going through a rock-bottom situation.

Spirituality looks different for everyone. You might go to church, temple, or mosque. Maybe you meditate or practice yoga. I find peace in reading the ecstatic poems written by Jalal ad-Din Muhammad Rumi, a Persian poet and Sufi master. When I take a moment to read his poetry, it brings me to a different place. One of my favorite short verses from Rumi is, "Out beyond ideas of wrongdoing and right doing, there is a field. I'll meet you there."

People in a relationship or a family may decide that they're going to practice their spirituality in different ways. Then, when they come back together as a family, they're going to be present because they gave themselves that gift of presence for themselves and their spiritual practice.

It's important that you have that freedom to practice your own spirituality without judgment—from yourself or others. It doesn't matter how you practice, as long as you are able to do so if it's important for you and fuels your soul.

A big part of your spiritual practice may be the sense of community you find with the other people who practice as you do. When you're able to tap into that group, it helps you feel less alone. You're connected with other people in your community, so you're not focused on your problems. Connecting with others helps you get out of your rock bottom for a bit.

What does your spiritual practice look like? What might you like to add or change? Maybe you want to read a prayer or make a gratitude statement with your family. You can create your own traditions. The most important thing is that when you're going through something and you need your practice the most, whatever you've set up in your life helps you. Your spiritual practice gives you a way to get centered through the ups and downs and realize you're not alone.

SET YOUR INTENTIONS

When we put our intention on something, whether in prayer, in a song, in meditation, or in reading poems, it creates a shift in the object of our focus. When your intentions are positive, it puts you in a better state of mind as well. It becomes easier to resolve the situation that is outside of you. You're in a better state to see it, even if you're still not fully in control of what happens.[2]

---

2   You can check out this video on Mindfulness for Health and Well-being from UCLA's Mindful Awareness Research Center for more information: https://www.youtube.com/watch?v=ilzc3gsIHos.

A study, referred to as the Ikea Plant Bullying Study, was done on two groups of houseplants: both were watered the same and had the same light, but one group was bullied and the other was loved. The plants that were bullied were all wilted and dying and sick looking. The houseplants that had heard positive words were beautiful and healthy.[3]

Whether that energy comes externally or internally, when we set our focus on the positive, more positivity shows up. That's not to say that it's healthy or wise to completely ignore a negative situation, though. It is often most productive to follow the BOOTS Formula with the negative situation and take the right action steps required. Then you can spend the balance of your time on the positive, because that's where the magic of life happens.

Our intentions and the thoughts and energy we send to people are felt. In Dr. Masaru Emoto's study on Water, Consciousness, and Intent, he had people put their intention or thought—or you could even call them prayers—onto water across the country, and the actual molecular structure of that water shifted.[4]

You may have experienced the intensity of your thoughts without noticing. Have you ever thought about someone you haven't seen in a really long time and then you get a call after they've been on your mind all day? I recently had that happen to me with June, a woman from my yoga studio.

I was invited to do a yoga teacher training program at my yoga studio. June, another teacher at the studio, got very angry with

---

3   https://www.adweek.com/brand-marketing/
    ikea-bullied-a-potted-plant-while-encouraging-another-then-showed-schoolkids-the-impact/.

4   https://thewellnessenterprise.com/emoto/.

me because she didn't like the car I drove. In her mind, the fact that I drove a Mercedes SUV wasn't very "yoga." Apparently, it's not spiritual to have a nice car. She either didn't know or didn't care that I had six kids I needed to fit in my car, and it needed to have good airbags. I was less concerned with the status symbol and more focused on the safety of my children.

I sent June some videos of monks in India who talk about spirituality and money. Their stance is that you don't have to suffer. We're all blessed in our own ways, and if you're grateful for the beautiful things that show up, there's nothing wrong with material comforts; it's what you do with what you have that's more important.

June wasn't having any of it. The next time I saw her, she yelled at me and then stomped out of the studio.

I acknowledged that her anger was her problem and I didn't own it; I was teaching yoga as a fun expression. Yoga's supposed to be about peace, love, and union. I didn't feel that at this studio, so I decided to stop teaching there.

Soon after that, I went on the travel tour with my children. We had many beautiful experiences, and then, when we returned, I went back to the little town where the yoga studio is. I did a class and didn't see June. I went home thinking about her and mentioned her to my daughter.

Suddenly, I had a beautiful, heart-opening moment of gratitude for June. In that moment, I understood the gift she had given me: she pushed me out of yoga as a training because I was supposed to take my kids on a world tour. If she hadn't had that issue with the car—that really had nothing to do with us—we might not have received all the beautiful things that happened that year. She might not have known, but that was pure love. That trip blessed our family so much more than teaching yoga.

As soon as we acknowledged that gift—this gives me chills—the phone rang, and it was June! We were joking about how silly she was, but the moment we acknowledged the gift in her push, she called.

June said that she'd seen on Facebook that I had started consulting. She said, "I'm having relationship issues. Can you help me?"

We hadn't spoken in those years—but, after that, we became close friends. After all, she was the one who pushed me off the yoga mat (not literally) and out into the world to do what I'm supposed to do.

You might be in a disconnect or a disagreement with a child or a loved one, and maybe the only way you can participate in that relationship is just by sending them love. You can decide whether or not you want to, but I'm telling you—just like the potted plants that responded to positive and negative thoughts—they will feel it. There's something magical about it. It could be that your relationship heals. It could be that they simply feel it, maybe not even knowing it's coming from you, and that's all you needed to do.

SETTING SELF-CARE BOUNDARIES

When you are going through a rock-bottom situation, you are most likely being pulled in many different directions. So many people want your help and time and attention.

How can you help those people without losing yourself? You will need to learn to delegate and set boundaries.

Both delegating and setting boundaries are like muscles: if you haven't used them in a long time, it can be difficult to get started. Once you start using them again, though, it gets much easier.

Delegating takes some of that pressure off of you so that you don't feel like you have to do everything. That gives you the time to also do the things that refuel and re-energize you, so you can do all the things you need and want to do in your life.

We've talked about setting boundaries in other chapters, but I want to give you my best practice: when somebody asks you for something, ask yourself these questions:

- Is this serving my highest and best good?
- Is it aligned with who I am?
- Would I only be doing this to please people?
- Do I feel like I'm *supposed* to do these things—even if I don't want to?
- Or will this help bring me to the outcome I desire?
- Is it fun?

Many times, we will say yes to something because we think we're supposed to—or even because we think we're supposed to find it fun. If it's not really fun for you, though, why give up your time and attention to do that thing if you don't have to? You could be doing something else that fuels your soul—especially when you're going through a difficult time.

When someone asks you to do something, take your temperature. If you imagine saying yes to going to a dance party or a concert or going out to eat, how do you feel? Do you actually want to go?

If it's a special situation or something for your children, you may say yes to share in their joy. We all have things we *have* to do or *want* to do. But we all also only have so much time, so you have to defend those things—and set up boundaries for the things you don't have or want to do.

Boundaries are healthy. It's okay to say no to things you don't want to do. If saying an outright no is difficult for you, try suggesting an alternative that works for both of you. Rather than just saying yes and then regretting it the whole time or saying no and feeling guilty, look for and offer a solution that makes you both happy and meets both your needs.

You have to consider what is the highest and best use of your time and then set that boundary out of love for yourself. You would do whatever is best for your child or partner or best friend—so it's time to do what's best for you, too.

SETTING HEALTHY BOUNDARIES EXAMPLE: PETER VS. PAUL

Healthy boundaries are one of the most important things a person can have, for their own wellness and for the sake of others. Let's look at an example of two students who were visiting the United States on student visas. One of them, Paul, has strong boundaries and enjoyed his entire experience as a student in this country. The other student, Peter, suffered for most of his experience due to a lack of solid boundaries.

Paul decided to find himself and try film school on for size.

He saved up his money, quit his job, and did all the paperwork in order to spend an entire year in the United States studying film production. His parents had raised him to really go within and find his own answers. They also had rock solid boundaries, so when Paul announced he was leaving the country for a year they respected his decision.

As soon as he started his courses, Paul applied for an unpaid internship at a new production company. When he requested the contract, however—which he needed for his visa paperwork—the company refused to provide documentation of their offer. As soon as he heard this, Paul chose to seek employment elsewhere. Eventually, he landed a job with a major production company. That company had no problem ensuring that the terms of his internship work were spelled out in a contract.

At the end of the school year, Paul graduated from his courses with good grades and a fantastic letter of recommendation to present to any film company he wanted to work for.

Peter also decided to attend a film school in Hollywood. He had saved up enough money to get his student visa and pay for the courses. His family even agreed to help him out with housing expenses. He was excited to be able to learn from the top film industry professors, and he also decided to get work experience through an internship program.

Peter applied for a position he heard about from a friend, who referred him to an aspiring producer's new production company. They didn't have any paperwork for him. They verbally agreed that Peter would work as a student intern for the company for four months, at which time the producer would either hire him for pay or give him a letter of recommendation. He really wanted to do a good job for this producer, because he hoped to be able to stay in the country and work full time for this company someday.

Because he had never learned to set boundaries, Peter worked up to sixty hours some weeks—all without ever getting paid. He took on his boss's ever-increasing list of demands, and his studies began to suffer. Peter's family and friends said that the producer was taking advantage of him and his desire to work for a big Hollywood production company, but Peter didn't listen.

After four months were up, Peter was failing out of film school and risked losing his student visa. The promised paid position never materialized. After warning him again and again, his parents cut off their funding. Suddenly, Peter could no longer afford to work without getting paid. He told the producer of the situation, and she promised to pay Peter for his work, but the check was always "in the mail." Somehow, that mail never came.

Peter failed out of film school, was kicked out of his apartment, and could no longer legally stay in the US. He had to move back home in shame, where he lives in his parents' spare room (which is, of course, really his childhood bedroom).

These are fairly extreme examples, but who would you rather be: Peter, who slunk home in defeat, or Paul, who succeeded at his goals? The only difference between the two is learning to practice strong self-love by setting effective boundaries.

APPLYING THE BOOTS FORMULA TO SELF-CARE

It may seem counterintuitive to use a formula to relax, but each step of BOOTS can help you take better care of yourself.

BEING

This first step asks who are you Being, but here we want to look at not only who are you Being for all these other people, but who are you Being for *yourself*? Who are you showing up as for yourself?

Are you treating yourself the same way you would treat a loved one?

Be honest, loving, and gentle with yourself. Ask for help when you need it—or even if you just want it. Be realistic about what you're going through, and remember that you get to decide how you are going to show up, so show up with lots of love for yourself, too.

ORIENTATION

When you look at any situation, it's not better or worse than it is; it just is what it is. If you find yourself focusing on self-care, perhaps after an extended time of focusing on others instead of yourself, you have choices to make—and you need to be honest about where you're starting from and where you want to go.

If you are rebooting or reinventing your life after a difficult situation, it is going to take a little bit of time to start seeing and feeling the benefits. Although you may feel a little more rested or just happier initially, the steady improvements will come with time.

When you first start making sure that you get time for yourself each day, it's not a habit. It may be difficult to set boundaries, or you may feel guilty about giving yourself time off to meditate or sing or do whatever self-care practice you choose. You are still getting this new habit of positive self-care built into your life.

Then, one magical day, you stop struggling and realize that you have finally reached equilibrium. From here on out, positive self-care is a pattern that brings you energy, wellness, and strength.

ORDER OF OPERATIONS

When you're going through something, it's very important to ask for help. Once you've evaluated where you are and where you want to go, you may not be able to get there on your own. The first step in your Order of Operations may be to get help evaluating what your next step is—and that's all part of self-care. You may be able to do everything, but that doesn't mean you should have to.

You also get to choose the order that makes sense for you, in your life. Maybe something has to go right now—and that's okay. Maybe you give one thing less attention so you can give yourself more. Maybe your house isn't as tidy as usual because you're moving and packing or unpacking right now. That's okay, too.

You have to make those executive decisions yourself. And once you make them, you have a better idea what the outcome's going to look like. Just the fact that *you* are in charge of it is very empowering.

THINKING

When you are Thinking about self-care, it's important to give yourself the same thought that you would give to anybody else. What would you tell a best friend to do? It should be that exact conversation, only with yourself.

You know what you need to do a lot of times. You already have it; you just have to put yourself in the right frame of mind—your Thinking mind—to envision what it's actually going to look like. What is your life going to look like tomorrow if you give yourself this meditation or prayer time today? What will happen if you go try that thing you've always wanted to do? What vision do you get when you think about taking an hour to journal or walk to the grocery store and make a healthy meal or jump on your bike? See in your mind's eye what that could look like and what results you might get—because the outcome is most likely going to be better.

That's true when you give that advice to a loved one, and it's true for you, too.

STEPPING UP

With self-care, Stepping Up is often the fun part. Step into what you've always dreamed of doing. Step into journaling or singing or gardening.

Get an accountability partner if you need one, someone you can send pictures to or update with your progress and who can cheer you on. Creating that system of accountability can really help with Stepping Up into it.

If you tell them, "Well, I didn't do it today," they can remind you that that's okay. But they can also let you know if they see you going back into the pattern of not giving yourself enough time for self-care. Their insights can help you get back on track.

There will be days where you're not going to be able to do everything you want to do. After spoiling yourself and practicing self-care for at least seven to ten days, however, you will feel like you can't *not* do it because it feels so good!

You will get better results in the rest of your life and have something to look forward to. You may even wonder why you didn't start doing this years ago. You will see the light!

FROM SELF-CARE ROCK BOTTOM TO MOMENT OF EMPOWERMENT

Lisa would walk on fire for her family and friends. She would never let anybody down—but she was letting *herself* down.

After she realized that she was going to become her own best friend, however, she saw the gift she was giving herself. She was going to show up and be who she needed to be for herself, because she was the one who needed the care this time.

Lisa also had to orient herself around the move she was making, which wasn't better or worse than it was; it simply *was*. It was a beautiful place to retire, but she felt alone. That's where she found herself.

She had to be honest as she looked at the reality of her situation. She had to decide what she was and wasn't going to do. When it came time to move, she had to evaluate not just what that would take but also ask, "Can I do this?" She made the choice to move, and now she has many new friends. But she had to change and adjust in order to do this once she decided it was what she wanted to do.

For Lisa, the Order of Operations was getting help with the move, giving herself time to rest and go through the grieving process while she was making this shift. She had to prioritize what she needed to do—but she also had to be vulnerable and honest enough to ask for help when she needed it.

In the Thinking stage, it was hard for Lisa to focus clearly because she was grieving, so I asked her to pretend that her husband was with her and sending her love. I asked her, "What would he gift you? What would he want for you right now? What would he be so happy to see you doing?"

So she took herself on dates and did things they would do, and she got through some of her grieving—but she also gave herself a break one moment at a time. It took her away from her situation, and it gave her time to heal. She gave herself permission. It was a challenge at first, but then you couldn't stop her.

She went shopping and picked out something for her new place. She went to see a musical with a friend of hers. She went on a three-day meditation retreat in Ohio. She took up gardening, because she'd always wanted to try it.

That filled her up again. Now she has friends where she lives, she likes it, and she volunteers. Her son comes to visit her regularly, and he's so happy to see her so happy and fulfilled. But she had to fill herself up in order to have enough love and time to give to others.

Re-BOOT Activity: Self-Care Rituals

Positive self-care is an intentional practice to stay balanced while meeting personal, physical, mental, spiritual, or emotional needs.

Self-care gives us the time to plug in and recharge, fueling our day or week for all the other activities we do.

Creating a regular ritual of self-care helps you stay balanced and energized, keeping you in a state of wellness so that you are able to easily handle the ups and downs in life.

Here is a checklist of fun, positive self-care activities. See how many you can complete for beautiful, authentic you, over the next ninety days.

- ☐ Do a random act of kindness for someone.
- ☐ Go for a walk by yourself with headphones on, listening to music you love.
- ☐ Prepare a healthy, nutritious meal for yourself or someone you love.
- ☐ Create something for no practical purpose, just for you, such as creating a song, a poem, an essay, a painting, a drawing, a comic strip, or a collage.
- ☐ Start a genuine conversation with someone you care about that covers the following: things that are going well, things you're having a hard time with, and things you are grateful for.
- ☐ Lay on the floor on your back with your eyes closed for five minutes (or longer) and just breathe.
- ☐ Shower with all the lights off. It forces you to move slowly, and it's so relaxing. Make sure to have safety mats in place so you don't slip on your way out.
- ☐ Stare at your pet or another animal and seriously contemplate their existence. Do you think they believe they have a higher purpose?
- ☐ Rearrange all of your furniture in a way that makes you more comfortable or just to try something fresh in your living space.

- ☐ Check in with yourself a few times each day and do a positive redirect to a favorite affirmation. Example: Change, "This work will never get done!" to, "Every day in every way everything gets done and life gets better and better!"
- ☐ Swing on a swing set. Too many adults forget how much fun this is.
- ☐ Sing out loud!
- ☐ Make up a fun message or song as your outgoing voice message.
- ☐ Use a planner or a calendar to intentionally schedule "me" time.
- ☐ In the morning, listen to music that inspires and motivates you.
- ☐ Write a list of things you're grateful to have in your life and post it somewhere you can see it often. We have a tendency to focus on the negative, so remind yourself of the good stuff.
- ☐ Go through your closet and purge the clothes you haven't worn in years. Donate them to a charitable organization.
- ☐ Go to a support group meeting and share.
- ☐ Go to a support group meeting and listen.
- ☐ Listen to a podcast about something that interests you that you haven't yet explored.
- ☐ Tell your cat all of your darkest, craziest secrets. His or her nonchalance and snuggles will remind you that you're okay.
- ☐ Write a letter to your secret lover, and then read it out loud before sending or shredding.
- ☐ Dance at home with the music turned up, like no one's watching. It may scare your pets—or they may join in!
- ☐ Draw a hot bubble bath, light candles, and play beautiful music.
- ☐ Curl up on the sofa or bed with a good book.
- ☐ Create a vision board for each area of your life: Personal Life, Health, Wealth, Spiritual Life, Family, Business, and Relationships.

I have other resources for self-care in the resource section of this book, and the most current updates can be found on my website. My goal is to make sure that as you heal and design a regular rhythm of self-care on your terms, you can connect to as many resources as possible. I also have additional activities for you to strengthen your own self-care and create your own spiritual practices based on your preference.

🎁 *My Gift to You* 🎁

Dear Readers,

There are so many benefits to starting a new rhythm of your day with Meditation and Affirmations.

There are so many scientifically proven benefits of meditation:

- Reduces Stress. Stress reduction is one of the most common reasons people try meditation.
- Controls Anxiety. Less stress translates to less anxiety.
- Promotes Emotional Health.
- Enhances Self-Awareness.
- Lengthens Attention Span.
- May Reduce Age-Related Memory Loss.
- Can Generate Kindness.
- May Help Fight Addictions.

Sign up for a FREE *28-Day Guided Affirmations & Meditation Practice* audio at www.SheilaMacshow.com/28daymeditation.

CHAPTER 11

LIFESTYLE DESIGN

This chapter is going to look a little different than the other chapters. Instead of starting out with a rock-bottom moment and ending with that person's moment of empowerment, we are going to compare the lives of two women.

THE LIFE OF ANN

Ann was very athletic growing up. As a young adult, she was active and healthy and loved to exercise. She helped rescue animals, volunteering at the local shelter to share her love with those animals.

Then she got married and had kids. Ann gave up a lot of her passions and the things that made her happy in order to please everybody else. Her husband is allergic to animal dander, so she couldn't have pets at home, and she gradually stopped going to the shelter, too. She didn't stay as active as she'd been when she was single.

She said yes to all her friends, doing anything they asked her to. She cared for a lot of people, but she didn't set boundaries. Ann's days were long and busy, full but not fulfilling.

Ann had had a vision of how she wanted her life to look, but she woke up one day and realized that she was living a very different life.

Eventually, Ann's health failed. She developed many health issues because she had stopped eating healthy foods, exercising, and taking time to rest her mind. She spent a lot of money on healthcare instead of spending time staying healthy.

When she really needed people to help her, she didn't know

how to ask. Some of her friends had more boundaries than Ann, so they said no to her requests—even though in the past she had helped them move or with accounting or babysitting. People weren't willing to give as much as she had, so she was at a loss. And with some of the people in her life who did want to reciprocate, Ann wasn't able to be vulnerable or gracious enough to receive.

Ann is at the point of retiring from a job she doesn't love, and she's physically and financially unable to keep up with her friends and family. She sees her friends doing work they're passionate about and talented at, and it affects her self-worth when she compares her life to theirs. She feels stuck, upset, and resentful. And she's angry with herself for letting life slip by.

Ann thought she was doing the right things. She was a good student, a good daughter and sibling, the one who didn't need so much attention. She was taught to put everybody else first. And she's done an amazing job of teaching everybody else to treat her like a doormat.

She never filled up her own self, and now she has a very painful void in her life.

THE LIFE OF BARBARA

Barbara has designed her life and lives it by her design. She has still done things for other people, but she follows her own definition of happiness and success.

Interesting things happened in her childhood, but, at some point, she decided that she was going to live life on her terms.

Barbara made a lot of mistakes. She tried to live her passion three or four different times in different ways. It didn't work out at first, but she was determined. At first, she wasn't even sure what that looked like, but she knew it would involve art, dance, and educating children. As it unfolded, she started teaching children to read and created a story-time program.

Looking back, she laughs about her ups and downs. The determination to live her life and work around her passion and her gifts was considered nontraditional, so she experienced some bumps that made her strong and resilient.

Barbara has kept solid rituals, routines, and boundaries in place. She eats healthy foods and takes care of herself, so she can help other people, too. She made her self-care a priority, knowing that she was modeling that for her children.

Barbara and Ann are the same age, but Barbara looks much younger because she's healthier and happier. She wakes up in the morning and is excited to go to work. When Barbara looks back at her life so far, she's at peace. She knows she's done her highest good. No part of her feels that she wasted time on things that don't align with her values. She lives exactly the life she was supposed to: the life she chose.

And she's excited for whatever comes next!

YOU ONLY GET ONE

Ann has lived her whole life based on what other people wanted, whereas Barbara has lived life for herself—and it's still full of love and other people. Which life would you choose? Maybe you choose a little of each. These are extreme examples, so maybe you choose neither. The point is that it's your life and you get to choose what it looks like.

Ann didn't choose to design her own life—but it's not too late. It's not over for her. It doesn't matter what your age is; until you're not here anymore, you can still make a change. The rest of your life can become the best part of your life.

All the decisions you make have an impact on your future, on your whole life. They build upon each other.

If you don't decide how you're going to live your life, somebody else is going to decide for you—and most people are happy to do that. They're happy to sell you the wrong house, so they can make a commission. They're happy to put you in a job you don't like for less pay, so you do all the work. But if you're not happy, it's not a blessing.

I'm not a Christian Scientist, but Mary Baker Eddy—the founder of the Christian Science movement—said, "Whatever blesses one blesses all."

If you're not happy, or if you're not living your essence, your truth, your *life*, it's hard for you to send happiness to other people in your life. But when you are happy and using your talents and gifts, there's no competition. There's no ego. You're just connected to everything and everybody in love, and it's beautiful.

Everyone has that beauty in them, in the way they're here and who they are. We're all amazing, talented, beautiful, incredible people in our own right.

When we try to shift and fit into a mold of who we believe we're supposed to be—the adult who never plays, who goes to work and takes on debt to buy a house—it kills our souls. Every day, we lose sight of who we really are.

How can you be happy when the most important parts of you are hidden or quieted because you've followed somebody else's rules?

How many people have felt like they had to go to school to become a doctor or a lawyer just because their parents wanted them to? And they're miserable! If they were living their truth, they would be happy—and that's worth even more than money. That allows them to attract the right peer group and a partner who's aligned with their truth.

It may sound obvious, but when you're not living your truth—you're living a lie.

When that's the case, you may say that you want something, but it doesn't align with you because it's not real. And you can't fake a life and a lie for long. The real you—the beautiful, amazing essence of you—is going to escape every time.

FREE YOUR SOUL

It's time to free your soul.

Start by figuring out your temperament, talents, and what you really love (you can refer back to the Re-BOOT Activity in chapter 6 to get started). There are surveys and tests you can take, but you have to be honest with your answers—so honest it may even hurt other people's feelings, like the parents who always dreamed of you becoming a doctor while you want to be a cruise ship comedian.

Doing this will free your soul to go be who you're really supposed to be. And when you are living the life you're supposed to, you're going to help people in your own way. You're going to live your purpose, because that's just who you are.

When you're fully living, you're able to fully contribute to society. Although you're doing more self-care, although you're just living your truth and your essence on your terms, you're going to serve far more people.

Taking care of yourself is not selfish. Finding your truth and designing your life based on that truth and your passion serves a higher purpose and a higher good. It serves humanity far more than doing what you or others believe you're supposed to do, so it's actually the least self-centric thing you could ever do.

SHEILA'S STORY

When my kids were old enough to go to school, and I was making cash flow from renting out the buildings my stores were in, I decided I wanted to be more involved. I wanted to be there with my children.

I'd taught the kids at the store. I'd led classes on safety and training. So I decided to get a teaching certificate to teach in private schools, mostly creative, art-centered schools such as Montessori and Waldorf. It was important to me that they were in this environment that featured learning through story, music, art, and their imaginations. I wanted them to learn languages, hand work, gardening, woodwork, and living through the history of different world cultures instead of just reading about them in textbooks. These private schools emphasize feelings and emotions, and the teachers are empowered to modify learning for each child. This unique standard of education was what I wanted for all of my kids—and I wanted to be there, too.

I had three children of my own and three foster kids—that adds up to a big tuition cost, but as a teacher my children would get to go to the school where I taught for free or at a reduced rate.

As a teacher, I felt like I got paid to have fun. I even started a tutoring program at my house, so I made a huge career shift from owning and operating stores to teaching—but I still showed up as myself. I was still me, using my capabilities and talents, and I was emotionally ready to make that shift.

I wanted to have as much time with my children as I could and be involved in their lives. The fact that I was being paid to be near them, and able to contribute to other kids, made teaching a natural fit.

I was doing life on my terms.

I was still getting income from my investment building. I never felt like I worked for somebody else—even when I did—because I was showing up on purpose, with a heart, a vision, and a reason.

The bonus came when, because I was a teacher, we all had the entire summer off. We were on the same schedule, so I had the summer off, Christmas vacation, spring break. When I was running the store, I didn't take a vacation for fourteen years. Now, I had the income and time with my kids, so we could go play. We could travel!

One summer, we went across the United States visiting all the historical sites. We would read about the Amish and then go see where they lived and learn even more. The culmination of our trip across the country was going to Epcot Center and feeling like we saw the rest of the world. We would study another culture, and then go learn about it at Epcot—it wasn't all rides and Mickey Mouse at Disney World!

APPLYING THE BOOTS FORMULA TO LIFESTYLE DESIGN

Using the BOOTS Formula, you can go from being stuck saying yes to everyone to becoming the woman you want to be.

BEING

Designing your life starts with the first step: Who are you Being?

That is going to be different for everybody. And once you've done some assessment to find your temperament, talents, and truth, you can look at how you are different from anybody else. Who are you going to be when you show up now? Who do you need to be, to truly be the best version of yourself? How are you going to live your essence and truth?

You may have a whole life set up around something that is not true to who you are. Now that you are redesigning your life—whether this is your difficult situation or you're doing so after making it through another rock-bottom situation—the gift is being able to set a new foundation. But that means knowing who you're going to be.

ORIENTATION

With this Orientation, you need to say, "This is where I am, and this is what I want."

What do you want your life to look like in a year? What do you want it to look like in five years? Most people overestimate what they can do in one year, but they underestimate what can be done in five years.

This is a complete lifestyle redesign. You're not just switching one thing or dealing with one emergency situation; you're reconfiguring every system in your life.

ORDER OF OPERATIONS

The first step in the Order of Operations is to figure out your first priority. If you could just do one thing today that would make everything else easier and make you feel really happy, what would that be? Giving yourself the time you need to think about and do this one thing will make you feel like you took care of yourself, and your whole day will be better.

Give yourself those little things—and they might be different each day. They build up, and when you consistently do the first thing you added, you can then add more things, and those build up too. Take it in order of priority.

You may need to adjust your relationship or get out of a career that doesn't serve you. That takes time. You're not going to make this choice and then be in the exact life you desire the next day. There are steps in between.

If you're not good at the steps, you may want to have somebody help you through that. You may be really great at seeing the vision, but you're not sure how to unravel all those pieces. Or you may be able to see little pieces but you're not quite clear on the vision.

You may need to give yourself a little bit more time than you think. If you make a one-year plan and a five-year plan, it may feel like nothing is changing at first. It's subtle. But once you start building, you get to a point where it gets easy. And the fact that you're not waiting to live your life on your terms is so beautiful and freeing and such a wonderful gift to yourself that you won't care if it does take five years to get the whole vision of what you want because you're already living it now. You're not giving that happiness to any other person, situation, or thing.

It could be that you're in your career still and you're going to switch over slowly. But how can you incorporate your true essence, talents, and truth in what you're doing today? Can you volunteer or start a side business so that you're actually having that happiness and fulfillment now, instead of waiting for a future perfect moment in time?

THINKING

Thinking is your mindset. It's setting your intention. And with that comes gratitude.

If you're starting over and rebuilding, but your budget doesn't allow for the fancy house or new car that you want, or if you can't start your desired career tomorrow, how can you adjust your mindset and be grateful for what you *do* have? How can your way of thinking guide you to enjoy where you are now?

Your environment matters—not just the furniture and the decorations but the energy that fills it. The energy—positive or negative—comes from the people around you, how the objects you surround yourself with make you feel, and the words and images you expose yourself to on the radio, television, and internet.

How are you setting up your home? How are you setting up your environment? If you have stress in your office or home, what can you do to shift away from that negative energy?

I went to the nail salon, and the news was blaring on the TV, full of war and death and horrible things. I don't want to be bombarded by that negative energy when I'm trying to relax. I know these things happen, I read the news and keep up with current events, but when I'm trying to rejuvenate and take care of myself, I don't want to see those vivid pictures that leave me feeling drained. I have friends, though, who love the news and can't work without it on.

Where can you create a sanctuary in your home? Sometimes just removing the television from your bedroom switches the whole energy. It could be as simple as moving things around to create a sacred space in your house where you can have that thinking time to draw, journal, or write your life vision.

You can design an intentional lifestyle that supports your individual rhythms. Once you see it and think it, start acting as if you already have it. You're going to live your best life today in gratitude. You're going to stop waiting to live. As you design your life, you're already in a better mindset.

STEPPING UP

Stepping up is your action step.

You are redesigning your life, so you're going to be different. Maybe you recreate your image and go get a haircut, color your hair, or change the way you dress. Maybe you redecorate your house or office. Maybe you are still working at your old career but you start doing volunteer work related to your passion. Whatever it is, just show up and do it. No waiting.

Start small, but step into that new thing.

My friend Ellen rode horses for many years but stopped after she had children. "I can't afford it," she told me.

So we looked at how to make it happen. I asked her, "Where's the closest place you can go? What options do you have?"

After contacting a stable, Ellen started going to groom the horses once a week, just to connect. Then she was able to trade grooming and cleaning for riding time. Eventually, she started teaching. Opportunities present themselves, but she had to physically be there to find them. She had to step into it.

There was a way—there's always a way to step into doing it, even if it's volunteering. If you want to get into shape, go take or teach the classes, work out with a fitness video on YouTube. If you want to meet new people, go to social events like book clubs or community cleanups. You're not going to meet them at home.

If you want to change your image and have people view you differently, mix up your outfits or change something about you as part of your redesign so your appearance is more in alignment with who you want to show up as. Have you ever noticed that when you dress up nicely, you show up differently? You feel better, even if the situation is the same—the only thing you changed is how you show up.

Be grateful for what you have and step into what you want, even if it's just for today. Tomorrow is going to get a little better, one step at a time.

MOMENT OF EMPOWERMENT: FIND THE GIFT IN YOUR SITUATION

This is the perfect time to reinvent or redesign your life. A difficult, terrible situation has happened, but now your new life is ready—and there was a gift in your rock bottom. Once you find the gift in a situation, your problems start to dissolve. It's like magic!

The silver lining in the cloud is that now you get to redesign your life. Life has its ups and downs. Situations happen that we wish wouldn't. But when they do, we're left with a clean slate. We're starting over.

Starting over is such a gift. Yes, you went through hell. You didn't want to go through that stuff. You didn't want to have a serious illness, get divorced, file bankruptcy, or have a loved one die. It was hard. But it served a purpose, and now you get to design your perfect life, your vision, and live on your own terms.

Sometimes in the storm, in chaos, as you start redesigning your life—even if you're still healing or transitioning—you're pulled out of that situation a little faster because you know where you're going. Even if your situation wasn't in your control, you still get the gift of the opportunity to re-examine your life.

When you're going through chaos, it's empowering to find the calm in the center of the storm. If you get centered and see where you're going and start to design your life, then you can have more calm even though you still have to finish walking through that storm.

Knowing that it's really tough right now, but that shift is never going to happen again—or, if it does, you're going to be ready—gives you hope.

When hope shows up in your life, you reach a higher level of energy and vibrational frequency. When you have hope, you're not in survival mode anymore and you use that hope to live the life you want to live.

Prioritizing yourself makes a night and day difference. Stepping away from the rock-bottom situation allows you to clear your head and refocus, giving you the clarity to see some really good solutions because you're not focused on the negative and your to-do list. Once you're relaxed, you'll see clearly what you need to do.

Then later, you look back and see that you redirected how you were living your life. You got healthier and happier. You started doing all the things you had always wanted to do but kept putting off until "someday." You show up in gratitude and receive all that love energy.

That positive love energy clears the way for your new life. Give yourself permission to receive it and then give back the gift of gratitude.

The biggest healing comes from self-love. Say yes to yourself and to what your heart really desires.

Activity: Design Your Dream Week

Sometimes we wish for the perfect week: a week straight out of a dream, one where only the very best version of you shows up. You go to sleep on time, you wake up feeling refreshed. You follow your healthy routine, take time for your wellness, and have amazing quality time with the person you're in a relationship with, your children, or your pets. You even get around to making those calls that keep getting pushed farther and farther down your list.

Sounds perfect, doesn't it?

A week like that is magic. You're able to do it all. At the end of every day, you sleep soundly, content in knowing that you got *all* of the magic juice out of each day. You showed up as your personal best. You may not have gotten absolutely everything done, but you feel proud of doing everything you could do. And you know that you're going to have another day tomorrow that will be aligned to your values and vision and your mission in life.

Days like that are easy. They don't feel like work. You have joy and pleasure in everything you do because you have that bright energy and purpose to your day.

Sound too good to be true? It's not, and I'm going to show you how.

1. The first step is to get out a piece of paper and something to write with—your favorite pen or pencil, if you have one.

2. At the top of the paper, write "My Aligned Week."

3. Down the left side, divide your paper into seven rows, one for

each day of the week.

4. Across the top of your paper, create six columns, and label them Family Life, Business, Social Life, Self-Care/Spirituality, Hobbies/Activities, and Purpose/Contribution. Make sure these topics are aligned with your ideal week, and if they're not, change them to reflect what's most important to you.

At this point, your paper will look something like this:

My Aligned Week

	Family Life	Business	Social Life	Self-Care/ Spirituality	Hobbies/ Activities	Purpose/ Contribution
Monday						
Tuesday						
Wednesday						
Thursday						
Friday						
Saturday						
Sunday						

5. Then, for each of these categories, fill in what's going to happen and on which day or days of the week. Maybe you want to have an hour every day with your children or spouse or taking the dog for a walk—write it in under Family Life on all seven days! How many hours a week are you putting into your career? Or, if you're retired, your volunteer work? Those go under the Business heading Monday through Friday (or whatever days work for you). Maybe you have a morning routine of meditation, yoga, prayer, or religious study. Fill in those days under Self-Care and Spirituality. This is your perfect week, and you get to design it any way you'd like!

6. Because this is your dream week, you can also add to it. Let's say you've always wanted to start a side-gig business or volun-

teer for the Humane Society or the Red Cross. In your perfect week, you get to do whatever you've always wanted to do but have never done. Maybe you do it for three hours that week, maybe every day. It could even just be twenty minutes of sketching in a business plan. In a perfect world where everything's aligned, how much time would you give to that passion-and-purpose business? If you want to improve something you're already doing, what would it take—a class once or twice a week? Online training? Fill in those dreams!

7. For each of the activities you are filling your dream week with, go back and also fill in how much time you'd like to spend on each one. Maybe you'd love to spend four hours every Sunday with family and friends. Your perfect week includes going to brunch and having fun, just playing. Put that in there!

8. You have this piece of paper, and it has these days and times and things you want to do in your perfect week. Now what? Well, the final step is to count up all the hours you listed. We all have 168 hours in our week. Subtract however many hours of sleep you need. Even if you dream of sleeping nine hours a night, that still leaves you with 105 hours to fill with your responsibilities—and your dreams! See where you actually have the hours in your week to make at least some of your perfect week come true. Maybe you can make 80 or 90 percent of it work. Maybe you have to cut back on some and make adjustments. But what I want you to realize is that you can start living what you consider to be your dream week. By next week, you could be living your dream. You could start today! What are you waiting for?

You will find other resources for Lifestyle Design in the resource section of this book, and the most current updates can be found on my website. My goal is to make sure that as you truly design the rest of your life on your terms, you can connect to as many resources as possible.

🎁 My Gift to You 🎁

As you go from rock bottom to back into action, there will be times when you have shown up for everyone else and you are NOW ready to reinvent your life and **need perspective** on your situation.

I want to show up for you. To ask me a re-BOOT question and receive a FREE GIFT of four weekly e-mails to help you through the lifestyle re-BOOT process, go to www.DearSheila.com. Please use a pseudo name and your favorite location so your question may be shared on the newsletter, and help others.

CONCLUSION

WELCOME TO THE SHEILA MAC SHOW: REALITY AT ITS FINEST

When I was a young kid, my parents got divorced. My mom was granted custody, and my grandparents forbade my dad from seeing me. His name was never mentioned, and I didn't see him again until I was a teenager, when a court contacted me—I hadn't even known he was alive until then. We reconnected when I was older; I was desperately looking for him at the same time he was frantically trying to find me, like our hearts were calling to one another. Before my father was diagnosed with cancer, he taught my oldest son how to play chess.

When I was younger, though, I lived with my grandparents and my mother. My mother had contracted polio as a young child, so she struggled to live and work independently. She also tended to be very emotional and somewhat childlike, often throwing tantrums or getting overly upset when things did not go as planned. But she was a beautiful lady, and it was her genuine optimism and youthful heart that taught me how to stay focused on the positive in life.

Unfortunately, a lot of unhealthy things happened in that home. My grandparents beat my mother, often throwing her into a wall and occasionally breaking bones. When I got older, I stepped in to prevent this abuse—and then I got beaten too.

Once, the police were called because of the noise. My grandfather was a reserve sheriff, and he said, "We need to teach her a lesson," and I ended up in juvenile hall.

I moved out of that house when I was eight years old, after stepping into the middle of another fight and ending up in the hospital with a concussion. I wanted to take my mother with me, to find an apartment and get her out of the house. I knew that if I could just move her out of that violence, everything would be peaceful and perfect. But I was young and the farthest I could go was sleeping in a metal shed in the back of our property. I was so happy to be in that damn shed, to be away from the abuse. It was cold in the winter and hot in the summer, but I decorated it for the holidays with paper chains and construction paper jack-o-lanterns. Kids are so resilient.

Most of my meals came from the neighbors who took me in and fed me. I did chores to help around their houses. They were aware of some of what went on at my grandparents' house, so they happily provided a safe place for me to visit.

At school, we were assigned speeches to write, and I wrote about freeing the hostages in Iran. I won our speech competition, and I got to travel around the country to other speech and debate programs. I was even invited to share my speech in front of President Carter!

Then, when I was eleven, the fighting showed up at the shed at five o'clock in the morning. My mom ran in and barricaded the door with furniture. "Go out the window," she told me frantically. "They're coming with straightjackets to lock you up!" I'd ended up briefly in the mental ward once before, with my grandparents telling me I was the crazy one, scaring me so I wouldn't say anything about the abuse. I didn't want to go back.

That's when I left for good, sliding out the window in my pajamas and running through the woods to the nearest bus stop.

I stayed with different friends. Because I needed a place to sleep, I became very social, fitting in with every group and clique in exchange for a warm bed or couch. Every day, I called my mom, just to tell her I was okay.

For a little while, I stayed with two friends from middle school in a small apartment in East LA. Their parents could barely make ends meet for their own family, and they couldn't afford to support me as well. After a week or so, the mom told me that I had to leave but that foster care was an option for me to be housed and fed. I'd never heard of it before, but she went with me and held my hand as I turned myself in.

I started in a Status Offender's Detention Alternative, or SODA, home in Pasadena. It was called Rosemary's Cottage, and it was basically a halfway home for kids coming off the streets. I stayed there for a few months until foster parents invited me to come stay with them in Covina. I loved staying there, but they were extremely religious and I felt like I didn't fit in. Eventually, I ended up in a group home—the David and Margaret Girls' Home—where I had more freedom, a full clothing allowance, and no parents telling me what to do.

A rich couple named Michael and Pamela—she was a famous artist, and he owned a hotel chain—bought the group home where I was living. Once I heard about that, I marched right up to their door, knocked as firmly as I could, and announced, "Hi, my name is Sheila Mac, and I want to be your personal assistant."

They hired me on the spot.

Michael and Pamela trained me to help them throw events and run their business. They gave me a room in their beautiful mansion-turned-art gallery.

Sadly, they eventually got divorced and, at age fifteen, I moved out again. I got an emancipation, finished high school early, and went out and started community college. I worked different office jobs, so I could afford my own place to stay. I had to support myself because I'd learned that no one else was going to.

That brings us full circle to where we started this journey: in the Introduction.

MAKING IT THROUGH

When I was very young, before I moved out of my grandparents' house, I would sit in the corner of the living room while my grandma met with a group of older ladies who were all businesswomen. These amazing, stoic, strong women came from all over the world and ran big businesses.

They would sit around the coffee table and tell stories of the hell they had gone through in their life journeys.

Mrs. Francis had spent the majority of her childhood in a concentration camp, and she told stories of how she lost touch with her parents and another lady took her in when they were freed at the end of the war.

Ms. Elaine told stories of growing up in Iran, living an incredibly elegant lifestyle. As a young girl, she was sent to boarding schools in France, and she spoke eight different languages fluently.

After she graduated, Ms. Elaine's parents married her off to an older man who demanded that she undergo female genital mutilation. Ms. Elaine told vivid stories of how badly her husband treated her. Then one day, her husband was in an accident that cost him his life. She admitted that she felt terribly guilty because she was secretly happy to be free of such a husband.

She returned to her family with nothing—except for a young baby. Eventually, they married her off again. This man, however, treated her kindly and they truly learned to love one another. Her husband ran a huge business in the plastics industry. She was treated like a queen, and her entire family was blessed by her marriage to this good man.

When the government changed to a different leader, they lost it all overnight. Ms. Elaine and her husband left all their worldly possessions and fled to the United States, where they had to start all over again. She never looked back, aside from the stories she would share around the women's table.

When the ladies told their stories, I felt as though I was there with them, living through the experience. I listened to every word. At five years old, I thought their adventures were amazing and I wondered what kinds of adventures I would have.

Even later, when I was alone and facing big rock-bottom issues in life, their stories gave me hope and a belief that if they could make it through their lives, I could make it through mine. I just knew that, no matter what happens, I would one day be an old lady who made it through, and I would be able to share my stories too.

All my life, I have tried to do the right thing—even when other people didn't. I believe in energy, in karma, in the gifts and blessings of this life. I look at every single step of my journey as a gift. There is a reason and a purpose behind everything.

Now my purpose is to share my gifts with you. To give you hope. To let you know that you are not alone on your journey. And to reach out and encourage you to tell your story, too.

THE JOURNEY

This may be the end of the book, but it's not the end of the road.

We are all continuing along our journeys together. One of the most beautiful parts about making a life shift is that you get to be among people who have gone through the same rock bottom as you.

All of us are women who love other people, who have gone through—or are still going through—something difficult. We pulled ourselves up by our boot straps and our bra straps, and now we're empowered to help other women. We know them because we've walked a mile in their boots. We recognize each other and say, "You wore those shoes, too!"

And now we're strutting in the sexiest red heels we can find.

Join the community to receive help when you're starting on your journey. Even at the beginning, sharing your story can help someone else, and you help yourself when you contribute.

Go to my website at www.SheilaMac.com. There is a lot of free material there, including activity sheets, resources, videos, and support groups.

I also have a "Dear Sheila" newsletter where those who are dealing with these different situations and life shifts write in for advice and answers to their questions. You've seen a few examples in this book, and if you have a question you'd like answered or if you're going through something, you can write in at www.DearSheila.com.

There is something for everybody. When you join the community of strong, powerful, beautiful women and incredible men Stepping Up to support the women in their lives, it will affirm that you are not alone.

As women, we can live in power. We are far more powerful together, when we support each other. When we care for each other. When we love each other.

When we wear our shoes, our boots, and our bras with pride.

We did it!

DIRECTORY OF RESOURCES

DEAR SHEILA NEWSLETTER

Dear Sheila,

My adult son David died recently in a motorcycle accident. His death was unexpected and shocking, and we are all heartbroken, especially his wife.

My son and I had a long discussion a week before we lost him. David informed me that he was planning to divorce his wife and wanted to build a life with his mistress, who is pregnant. He wanted advice on how to best tell his current wife and never got around to it. His current wife never wanted to have children, and now that our son is gone it puts me in a difficult spot. I have not said anything to my daughter-in-law, as we have all been grieving.

The mother of my grandbaby also attended the funeral, yet his wife was not aware at that time. I have been able to make friends with the mother of my grandchild; she is a great lady. Honestly, I love them both. I also feel a desire to be connected with our only grandchild, who is due in a month.

My dilemma is that I have not told my son's wife about the situation as she loved him dearly, and I feel it would crush her at this time. My question is, should I continue to hide the baby from my son's wife, or should I tell her about the situation?

—Torn between Two Lovers

Dear Torn between Two Lovers,

I am so sorry for your loss; one of the most challenging things to face is losing a child, even when they are adults.

My first question in cases like this would be to ask you what your son's wishes would be. From your question, it sounds as if your son was preparing to announce it to his wife before this tragedy struck.

Although the circumstances are not ideal, it would seem that honoring your son's wishes to expose his truth would be fair to both his wife and the mother of his child. Timing is critical, and you may want to have a person that is a close mutual friend or family member be present with your daughter-in-law when you share this difficult news.

Of course, your other option may be to distance yourself and move on. If you live near both ladies and are going to start sharing photos of your grandson online and such, telling the truth is tough, yet it is the kindest thing to do.

As always, I wish you,

"Life, Love, Laughter & Light!"

—Sheila Mac

📩 *Dear Sheila Newsletter* 📩
Answering Real Questions with Real Solutions to
Re-BOOT Your Life

Dear Sheila,

I am feeling extremely betrayed and confused. I have been a faithful wife married to the same man for twelve years with no children yet.

I went on a two-week business trip with my coworkers and had trouble reaching my spouse. Upon returning, I was greeted at the airport with a peck on the cheek, and after continuously trying to become intimate with my husband, he seemed very distant.

He finally told me that while I was traveling, he had a one-night stand in the mountains with some lady he met at a bar. My husband promised that it was over, and that fling meant nothing, he just drank too much, and things got out of hand.

Later that month, I found out my husband was continuing to have a relationship with his "one-night stand."

My question is, after twelve years should I give him another chance because we have been considering having children? Am I too untrusting, am I too old to start looking for another relationship? Was this his first offense?

—Betrayed & Confused

Dear Betrayed & Confused,

It is beautiful that you upheld your agreements and wish to come to amends with your spouse; that shows your integrity and love for your husband. It may be worth the expense to attend a couple's therapy program or do a relationship reboot challenge.

If your man agrees to talk things out with a neutral party, that may help you both decide which direction to take your marriage. On a personal level, you must put self-love into this equation and set the standard on what terms you would be willing to come to in your relationship. Such as: if your guy does continue to lie and cheat on you, at what point do you walk? Or are you willing to have an open relationship?

It could very well be your love has a drinking or addiction problem and needs some help, or that he is not ready in his life for a committed relationship. There are ways to love someone and still love yourself enough to get out of a relationship if things do not improve. I wrote an entire chapter about relationships that goes deep into this type of situation.

You are not alone, and your child deserves to come into the world with two loving parents if at all possible.

The most important thing to do is wait on having children until you and your husband reconcile, and your renewed marriage shows a good solid amount of healing time. A child is an even greater commitment, and if your man is not ready it would be much harder to leave with a little one in tow.

As always, I wish you,

"Life, Love, Laughter & Light!"

—Sheila Mac

📧 Dear Sheila Newsletter 📧
Answering Real Questions with Real Solutions to
Re-BOOT Your Life

Dear Sheila,

I am thirty-eight, and after being married for a few years, we finally had twins. After the babies were born, my husband and I became distant. Our love life started to fizzle and then for our anniversary, my husband and I agreed to do a threesome with another man to bring some excitement back into the bedroom.

We had never done this before, and I was delighted with the other man. I had never been so pleased by a lover. Now, I feel guilty and have continued a side relationship with our bed mate.

The issue I have is that my new love has offered to take me into his life and wants me to leave the marriage; yet I love my children and feel obligated to stay. I am conflicted and confused about what to do.

My question is, should I wait and go to couples' therapy or something of that nature, or move on to the man that truly floats my boat?

—Third Wheel Lover

Dear Third Wheel Lover,

Congratulations on your twins! It seems as though you and your husband have a very open marriage and yet are in a bit of a conflict on how to come to terms with the various roles you both agree to share together. Without intimacy, what you may have is an incredible friendship and now a family.

There may be more things going on here than emotional, and your experience with this other man may be related to your postpartum healing on a physical or even emotional/hormonal level. It would be a good choice to talk this over with your obstetrician as well as discuss openly with your husband about the type of intimacy you desire.

Perhaps you may both experiment with a knowledgeable sex therapist. This would be a good choice if you are happy in your marriage on all other levels. It is for you both to discuss and decide, as far as the type of relationship you will continue in, or if it is best for all concerned to agree to send love and move on. If you do part ways, as three open-minded adults it may be beneficial to come together on how to create a new form of co-parenting those little ones in love and freedom.

Creating your own type of family traditions and roles would be a very beautiful gift to your children.

As always, I wish you,

"Life, Love, Laughter & Light!"

—Sheila Mac

Dear Sheila,

I am a newly divorced female, age forty-three. I live in a small two-bedroom apartment by myself, and sometimes my daughter shares the space with me in between college semesters. I have a newer car and heavy car payments and live where the cost of living takes up the majority of my income.

I run a small accounting business and work odd jobs for extra funds in order to pay my bills. Work takes up so much of my time that my continuing education and social life has suffered. I also want to take some new courses on social media to market my company better.

I have low energy and can't seem to get ahead these days. I don't even have time or extra money for online courses, which is really frustrating.

I do have a newer boyfriend; we have dated almost eight months. We were close friends for a couple years before we started going out, during my separation. He's a great guy who also does tax accounting, mostly. His income is seasonal and so he currently is living with a roommate here in Southern California to keep his costs down.

The other night, he brought up the idea of us living together. I really enjoy his company, yet I have no desire to take our relationship to the next level. On the other hand, we would both benefit from reducing expenses and could see if living together would work, which may make or break our relationship.

My question? The truth is, I really would not consider my boyfriend for a roommate if finances were not the issue. I have thought this through and am still somewhat conflicted, as there seems to be no other options. There aren't any apartments that would cut my living expenses enough so I could quit my extra jobs or take courses to increase my business revenue.

I'm afraid if we live together it could be a costly mistake, yet if I continue the way finances are, I will never get ahead. Do you think it would be a mistake? Do you have any other suggestions that may work for us?

—Living California Style

Dear Living California Style,

It sounds like there are two separate issues here. One is deciding on the pace and place you want to move or not move to in your relationship. Since you both are working on building finances and covering costs, moving in together sounds nice.

The problem is that the reason is more about the finances than the actual love. Relationships take time, and often rushing into a living together situation puts a great deal of pressure on a couple if it is not coming from a space of complete comfort.

The beautiful part is that you have a wonderful new relationship in your life and you're both in a similar field. It may be a fun game to see if you could create a part-time accounting-based business together that would cover both of your extra expenses, give you time together and the space you need to get to know one another before making a commitment to move in with one another.

There is also your daughter to consider, as she stays over for visits often. What is your comfort zone and hers with having your new love move into her part-time space? There are also other adjustments you might make, such as refinancing or trading in on that newer car to a model and price that works for you.

Perhaps you could find a short-term roommate that is female or rent part of your home out on a vacation rental platform. Do not move in with a boyfriend if you are not ready for that step.

The fact that part of you was compelled to ask this question is a big part of your answer. When the relationship is ready for a real commitment or living-together arrangement, you will automatically not have to question it because the time will feel like the next right step for both of you.

As always, I wish you,

"Life, Love, Laughter & Light!"

—Sheila Mac

📧 *Dear Sheila Newsletter* 📧
Answering Real Questions with Real Solutions to
Re-BOOT Your Life

Dear Sheila,

I am a forty-one-year-old divorced mother of a happy pit bull named Freckles. I feel like I have hit a bit of a financial rock bottom. For the last few years, I have been spending a little more than I earn regu-

larly, and recently I found out I have a judgment from a debtor. The people I owe money to are constantly harassing me. I already work two jobs and am now struggling to keep up with Freckles' vet bills.

Before my divorce, I always had a stellar credit score and tracked every penny. Unfortunately, it has been challenging to switch to one budget, pay all the related attorney fees, and settle old debts. Now I'm considering filing for bankruptcy to have a fresh start.

My relatives are angry with me because they discovered my situation. Sadly, most of it was my ex-husband's purchases on joint accounts, and now I am saddled with both our bills. I keep getting notices in the mail and I have given up, so I just throw them into a big box because I don't have the money to pay them. What do you think I should do?

—Bankrupt for Freckles, Florida

Dear Bankrupt for Freckles,

The most empowering thing a person can do who is entangled with the debt monster is to face it. I know that often seems impossible; yet you are among thousands of people who also have hit a tough spot in life and need to get financially reorganized. The good news is that because this is a common symptom that shows up after dealing with a rock-bottom event, it is also a sign that a life reboot is imminent.

There are some easy fixes, and because this is very common, credit companies are more than willing to make reasonable arrangements with you. The first thing to do is actually organize all your bills. This will energetically show that you are now taking your power and life back. Open them up and then contact a few credit repair services for a free consult. These companies can refer you to a good attorney to advise you on the judgment and also review what else is showing up on your credit score.

Having a judgment is not a sign that bankruptcy is the only answer. Even if you need to wait on hiring a service, their free advice will be priceless. Credit repair companies can actually help you dispute incorrect information on your report, tell you if bankruptcy should be considered, negotiate payoff amounts to often half what one owes, and help you strategically rebuild your score.

The moment you accept the responsibility of these first few steps, the answers will relieve a ton of stress. Then, as you start to walk forward in your rebuilding, you will be able to also start creating ways to save up for Freckles. In the meantime, work out a payment plan with your vet as well. He or she will appreciate your call or letter, and in most cases will be more than happy to work with you on that plan and keep your little one as a patient.

There are also many veterinarians who offer a sliding fee scale based on need; ask your local humane society for some referrals. I have an entire chapter on finances and a formula to help you set up a strategic new life plan, so that this will be the last time this situation shows up for you and Freckles.

As always, I wish you,

"Life, Love, Laughter & Light!"

—Sheila Mac

Dear Sheila,

I am thirty-three years old and the mother of a two-year-old daughter. Married for four years, I recently found out that my husband was contacting a mutual friend named Chris.

When I inquired as to whom he was speaking with, he told me a work colleague; yet it was a mutual friend, Christina, that he works with.

After asking about all the sudden phone calls, my husband then said to me that he was seeking comfort in the arms of another and wanted to pursue a relationship with her.

Should I wait around for him to figure out what he wants, or should I file for divorce?

The fact that the relationship continues is too close for my comfort level. Would you advise me confronting Christina about this indiscretion and see how stable this other relationship is?

—Too Close for Comfort in Hawaii

Dear Too Close for Comfort,

Sometimes people do grow apart or spend more time in proximity with others and the line of friendship gets blurred into a relationship. It may be helpful to have some open discussions on why your husband felt he needed to seek comfort outside of the marriage.

Whatever he says, although it is important for your own growth to see your role or part in this, it usually has very little to do with anything you did or did not do as a wife. The open dialogue is very helpful in being able to either agree to start over and work together or to make a conscious and loving choice to move on and get a fresh start.

You also mentioned you share a child together, and that is why it is even more important to do your best to keep open lines of communication and work together on the common ground of how to best uncouple and continue to joint parent your two-year-old if that is the road you take.

It sounds like your spouse has made a declaration and brought his work relationship to your attention. The fact that he is being honest with you is far better than continuing to be in a marriage where he is not in truth.

Although walking away seems difficult and not convenient, living in a relationship that is based on lies is far more painful. Although your child is very young, the lessons in how you show up through this relationship shift will be an example of how to later get through his or her own tough times.

As always, I wish you,

"Life, Love, Laughter & Light!"

—Sheila Mac

✉ Dear Sheila Newsletter ✉
Answering Real Questions with Real Solutions to Re-BOOT Your Life

Dear Sheila,

I have a father who is an alcoholic as well as a marijuana addict. My dad sometimes acts out or is hateful and mean to my loved ones or me when he is high. I want to be a good daughter and love him through this issue, yet I am not sure how to connect with him after he does such cruel things.

Do you have any advice on how I can spend time with my dad, yet somehow get him to stop that behavior?

—Addicted to Family in Massachusetts

Dear Addicted to Family,

Dealing with a loved one with addictions can be so tricky. Support their efforts on kicking these drug and alcohol dependencies, acknowledge their successes—even if their success seems small. Be prepared with a list of support groups, doctors, and programs for any time your loved one asks for help.

Give the person information they may need to get further professional advice, yet in no way condone the using patterns they are repeating. Sadly, addiction affects so many people.

Since you are not under the influence, you are in a much healthier mental state than your dad is when he acts out. It is the nonaddict that must set the tone during this type of relationship. Choose how and when you will spend time with your father. If you know of times when he is more likely to be using, schedule a different day for a visit that will align.

Take a moment to write out a short list of what is and is not acceptable for your dad when he is around you and your family. Title it, "An Agreement to Myself." If at all possible, talk with your loved one when he is not in an altered state. Let him know what happened briefly and tell him in advance, if at all possible, what the consequences will be.

Say, "If you start cussing, we will have to leave immediately. We will return at another time when you are sober." Let the person with the addiction know that this will be the exact standard you hold with them, and be willing to follow through with whatever you say you will do.

If you cannot tell them in person, either write it to them or keep that in your heart and follow through on your new standards.

A person who is under the influence or struggling with addictions is not in their best mindset. If they were not in a drug-induced state, they would never want you or their loved ones treated so poorly. They are not well, and setting loving boundaries will help them and let them know you are always in control of how others treat you.

Addictions can be cured and overcome. Love the person and yourself through this with agreements and sometimes the gift of time for your self-care whenever needed.

As always, I wish you,

"Life, Love, Laughter & Light!"

—Sheila Mac

The following are resources you may find useful, broken up by chapters/rock-bottom situations. For additional resources, please visit www.SheilaMac.com.

CHAPTER 2: FEEL YOUR FEELINGS (GRIEF)

Honoring the time for grief, helping you walk and work through it, but not telling you to just get over it:

https://www.samhsa.gov/find-help/national-helpline

https://www.counseling.org/knowledge-center/
mental-health-resources/grief-and-loss-resources

https://www.helpguide.org/articles/grief/coping-with-grief-
and-loss.htm

https://www.centerforloss.com/grief/getting-help/

Activities and social engagement:

https://whatsyourgrief.com/reconnecting-with-life-after-loss/

Attend social gatherings at churches or social centers.

CHAPTER 3: SHIFT OR GET OFF THE POT (RELATIONSHIPS)

Redefining relationships in the second act of life:

https://www.huffpost.com/entry/
should-i-stay-or-should-i-go-self-assesment_b_5091106

https://www.narcity.com/dating/20-clear-you-should-stay-in-your-relationship-or-leave-asap

https://www.psychologytoday.com/us/blog/shift-mind/201610/should-i-stay-or-should-i-go

Activities:

https://getyourshittogether.org/checklist/

https://thestir.cafemom.com/love/172149/the_divorce_bucket_list_50

Join a book club: http://www.bookclubcentral.org/how-to-book-club/find-a-book-club/

Join MeetUp.com or create your own group and meet people near you who share your interests.

CHAPTER 4: THE MANY MASKS OF ABUSE

Sexual Abuse:

Stop It Now! prevents the sexual abuse of children by mobilizing adults, families, and communities to take actions that protect children before they are harmed, providing support, information, and resources to keep children safe and create healthier communities. Since 1992, we have identified, refined, and shared effective ways for individuals, families, and communities to act to prevent child sexual abuse before children are harmed—and to get help for everyone involved. https://www.stopitnow.org/help-guidance

The Rape, Abuse and Incest National Network (RAINN) organizes the National Sexual Assault Telephone Hotline. The hotline is a referral service that can put you in contact with your local rape crisis center. You can call the hotline at 1-800-656-4673, or access RAINN's online chat service at https://hotline.rainn.org/online

Domestic Violence:

National Domestic Violence Hotline: 1-800-799-7233 or TTY 1-800-787-3224. https://www.thehotline.org/resources/victims-and-survivors/

CHAPTER 5: MONEY MATTERS (FINANCES)

Support with having to manage finances, possibly dealing with losing or replacing an income:

https://cashmoneylife.com/financial-moves-when-laid-off/

https://primewomen.com/second-acts/new-surroundings/second-act-career-changes-for-women/

https://www.helpguide.org/articles/stress/job-loss-and-unemployment-stress.htm

https://www.debt.org/advice/budget/

https://www.ellevest.com/personalized-portfolios

https://www.daveramsey.com/

Activities:

https://www.practicalmoneyskills.com

https://www.thesimpledollar.com/
ten-simple-yet-life-changing-personal-finance-strategies/

CHAPTER 6: WORKING HARD FOR THE MONEY (CAREERS)

Different career shifts at different stages of life:

https://www.aarp.org/work/career-change/

https://www.themuse.com/
advice/7-things-to-consider-before-a-career-change

https://www.forbes.com/sites/kathycaprino/2019/04/13/
what-career-confusion-looks-like-at-three-key-stages-of-
life/#7fd3b99655b6

http://www.211.org/

https://www.takechargeamerica.org/

https://smartasset.com/retirement/
top-11-retirement-strategies

CHAPTER 7: YOU'LL ALWAYS BE MY BABY (PARENTING TEENAGERS AND ADULT CHILDREN)

How to have a healthy transition into the different relationships with grown children or with your parent as an adult:

https://www.empoweringparents.com/article-categories/
ages-and-stages/adult-children/

https://lifestyle.howstuffworks.com/family/parenting/
parenting-tips/10-tips-for-parenting-adult-children.htm

https://sixtyandme.com/
letting-go-and-the-art-of-parenting-adult-children/

Activities:

https://bestlifeonline.com/adult-children/

https://www.adventuresofemptynesters.com/
fun-things-to-do-with-your-adult-kids/

https://www.readers.com/
blog/5-activities-with-adult-children/

CHAPTER 8: PARENTING YOUR PARENTS (ELDERCARE)

Support in becoming the person responsible for making decisions, advocating for healthcare, and respecting last wishes:

https://www.caregiver.org/parenting-your-elderly-parents

http://www.eldercarelink.com/

https://www.apa.org/helpcenter/elder-care

https://www.agingcare.com/articles/10-government-

programs-caregivers-can-access-for-their-elderly-
parents-120513.htm

https://moneywise.com/a/
essential-documents-for-aging-parents

Activities and social engagement:

https://homecareassistance.com/blog/
science-social-engagement-healthy-aging

- Play games like Bingo with friends
- Go for a stroll in the park
- Better yet, have a picnic in the park
- Feed the ducks

CHAPTER 9: BREAKING THE CYCLE (ADDICTION)

How to deal with your own addictions or with loved ones who
are fighting to get out of a drug, drinking, or other addiction:

Alcoholics Anonymous is an international mutual aid fellow-
ship with the stated purpose of enabling its members to "stay
sober and help other alcoholics achieve sobriety." AA is nonpro-
fessional, self-supporting, and apolitical. Its only membership
requirement is a desire to stop drinking: https://www.aa.org/

Al-Anon members are people, just like you, who are worried
about someone with a drinking problem: https://al-anon.org/

SAMHSA's National Helpline, 1-800-662-HELP (4357),
(also known as the Treatment Referral Routing Service) or
TTY: 1-800-487-4889 is a confidential, free, 24-hour-a-day,

365-day-a-year, information service, in English and Spanish, for individuals and family members facing mental and/or substance use disorders. This service provides referrals to local treatment facilities, support groups, and community-based organizations. Callers can also order free publications and other information.

National Institute on Drug Abuse (NIDA) Research Programs and Activities: https://www.drugabuse.gov/research/nida-research-programs-activities

Suicide Prevention: The Lifeline provides 24/7, free and confidential support for people in distress, prevention and crisis resources for you or your loved ones, and best practices for professionals. https://suicidepreventionlifeline.org/ or 1-800-273-8255

CHAPTER 10: SELF-CARE AND SPIRITUALITY

How to take care of yourself while taking care of everyone else:

https://blogs.psychcentral.com/imperfect/2019/07/how-to-take-care-of-yourself-when-you-are-busy-taking-care-of-everyone-else/

https://chopra.com/articles/10-spiritual-self-care-tips-you-need-to-know

https://rebalancewellbeing.com/

https://tinybuddha.com/blog/45-simple-self-care-practices-for-a-healthy-mind-body-and-soul/

Activities:

https://www.goodtherapy.org/
blog/134-activities-to-add-to-your-self-care-plan/

Boundaries and Codependence:

How to use self-love and boundaries to reboot from a codependent situation and setting boundaries with family and friends:

https://www.cognitivehealing.com/personal-growth/how-to-develop-healthy-boundaries-in-codependent-relationship/

https://experiencelife.com/article/
no-boundaries-overcoming-codependence/

Activities:

https://psychcentral.com/
lib/10-way-to-build-and-preserve-better-boundaries/

CHAPTER 11: LIFESTYLE DESIGN

How to design your life based on your definition of happiness and success:

https://letsreachsuccess.com/what-is-lifestyle-design/

https://lifeskillsthatmatter.com/lifestyle-design/

https://www.forbes.com/sites/celinnedacosta/2018/07/31/3-ways-to-start-designing-your-dream-life/#171105f61253

https://www.wealthwelldone.com/lifestyle-design/

Activities:

- Daily meditation
- Go on a retreat
- Take up yoga
- Find a mentor that you can relate to

ACKNOWLEDGMENTS

To my beautiful, authentic, now-grown children: thank you for being my most gifted teachers.

To all the people who supported me and stayed by my side when the shift hit the fan, I thank you.

I also thank *me* for investing in my own personal development journey and gifting myself and my family many trips to educational and inspiring events and trainings. What a blessing it has been to be able to learn from such incredible leaders as Tony Robbins, Cloé Madanes, Dr. Wayne Dyer, and Jay Abraham.

I especially thank all the people on the planet who did their damn best to hold me back and make life difficult for me. I know they gifted me with strength, resilience, and lots of street smarts.

I also want to thank the editors and assistants who helped me get this out on a very tight timeline and the publishing company who believed in my vision for this heart-centered book even at its first draft. You gave me the fortitude to not give up on the process.

I acknowledge each and every woman who was guided to read this, as well as the men reading this to learn how to best help the women who matter most in their lives. Thank you for your trust and time. I hope that this book reminds you of who you really are, gives you the strength to reboot your life on your terms, and empowers you to know that you are not alone on your journey.

ABOUT THE AUTHOR

As a Southern California native, **SHEILA MAC** is no stranger to sunlight. However, her innate ability to find a glimmer of light in even the darkest of situations sets her apart from the rest. As a mentor with a focus on lifestyle reboots, it is Sheila's desire to teach all of her clients how to find that light as well.

Sheila is the parent of six beautiful children and has a passion for helping people succeed. For over twenty-five years, she has helped women take their lives to another level through solid lifestyle consulting and accountability programs. Sheila focuses on the ever-present opportunities before all of us and teaches her clients not only to seize said opportunities but more importantly how to recognize them.

Sheila Mac's unwavering dedication to being a lifelong learner has made her the successful entrepreneur she is today. Along with speaking engagements, online courses, and individual coaching, Sheila has also been a property investor and real estate team leader. Through her team at Keller Williams of Beverly Hills, Sheila still intuitively helps her clients invest in properties to fuel their dreams. She believes that no matter how successful they already are in the areas that matter most, their businesses, personal finances, intimate relationships, families, careers, and health are all affected by the investments they do or do not make.

Sheila is an expert on moving forward: She has spent her entire life growing an impressive spiritual and fiscal living from nothing. Her unique story allows her to connect with any client regardless of background in order to help them reach their full potential both personally and professionally.

CPSIA information can be obtained
at www.ICGtesting.com
Printed in the USA
LVHW112316170820
663477LV00008B/236/J